101 Things to do With a Mosquito

by
Ed Fischer

Adventure Publications, Inc.
Cambridge, Minnesota

To Gordon, without whose inspiration this extraordinary project would not have been possible.

Text and illustrations copyright 2004 by Ed Fischer

Book design by Jonathan Norberg

10 9 8 7 6 5 4 3

Published by Adventure Publications, Inc.
820 Cleveland St. S
Cambridge, MN 55008
1-800-678-7006
www.adventurepublications.net

ISBN-13: 978-1-59193-101-0
ISBN-10: 1-59193-101-0

Mosquitoes!

Those pesky pests! Most of the time you can't see them, but you can hear them. They buzz and buzz until 'yikes!' 'Gotcha!' You can swat them, spray on smelly stuff or zap them with electricity, but they still drive you nuts. Most outdoors people don't want to stink from repellent and you can't carry around a zapper with you wherever you go. The solution is in your hands. We say there are ways to control these varmints of the swamp. We say, laugh in their faces. That's what you'll do with this book by me, internationally renowned expert on mosquitoes that buzz in the back yards of 5th Avenue in northeast Rochester.

There are 101 things we can do with the mosquito. The sooner we get started, the better.

-Ed Fischer

Mosquito alarm clock

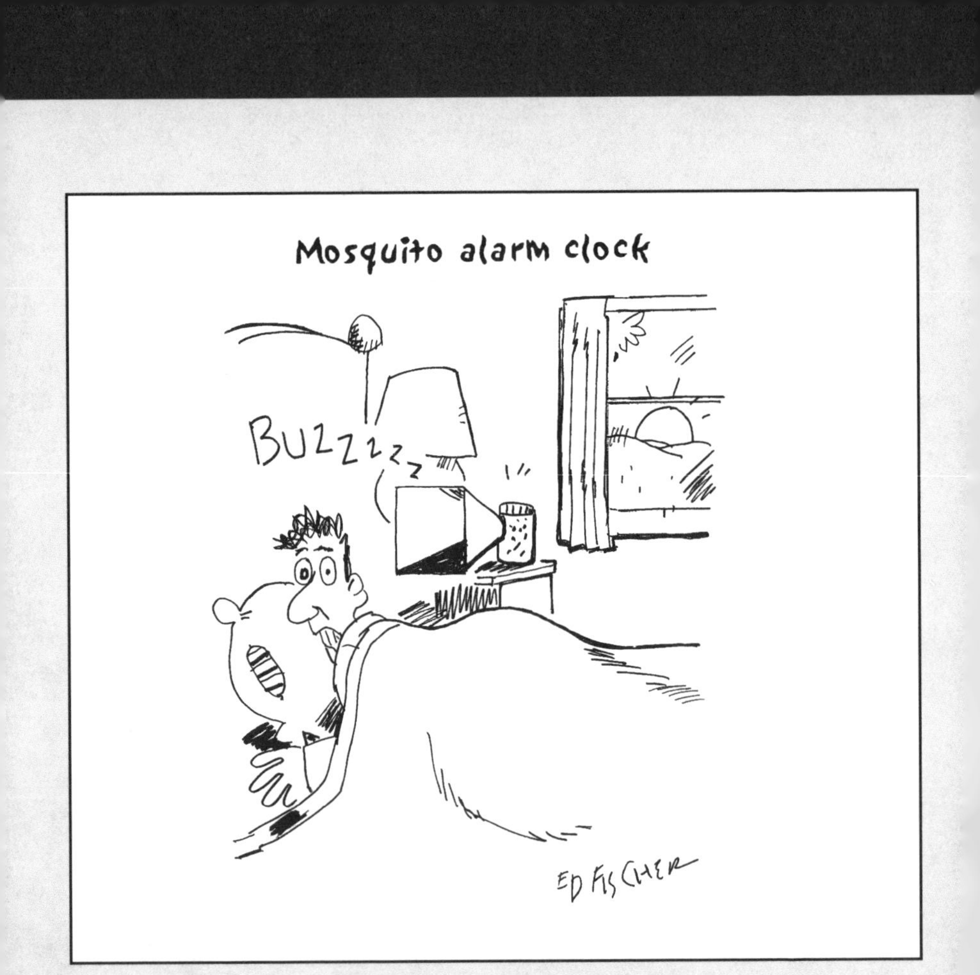
BUZZZZZZ
ED FISCHER

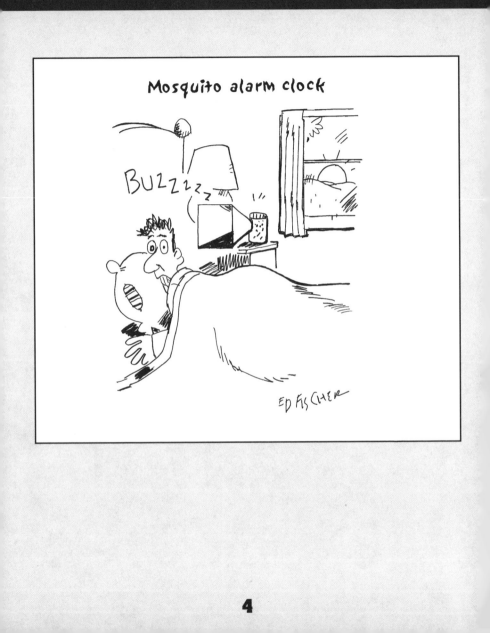

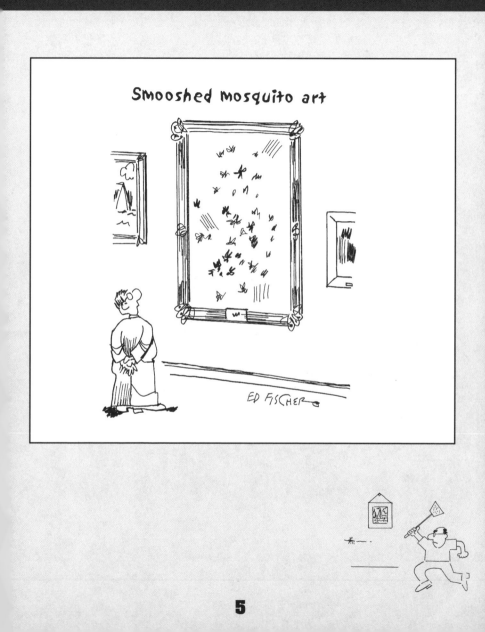

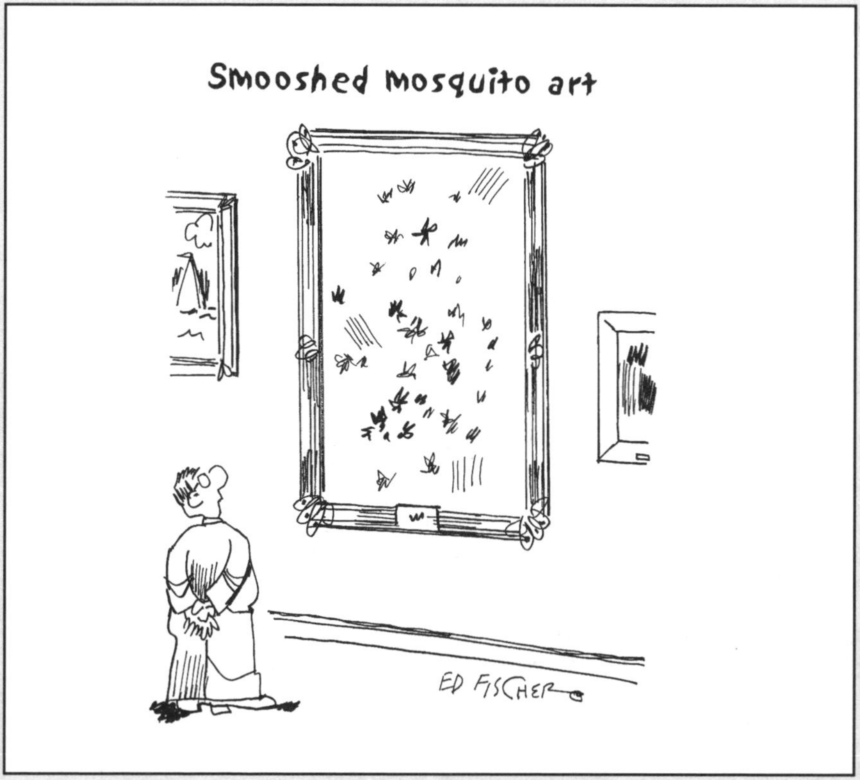
Smooshed mosquito art
ED FISCHER

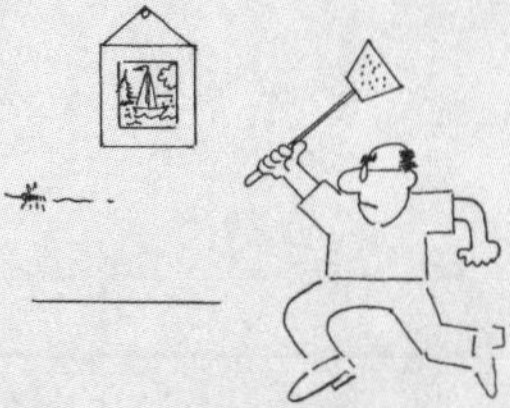

To get everyone's attention

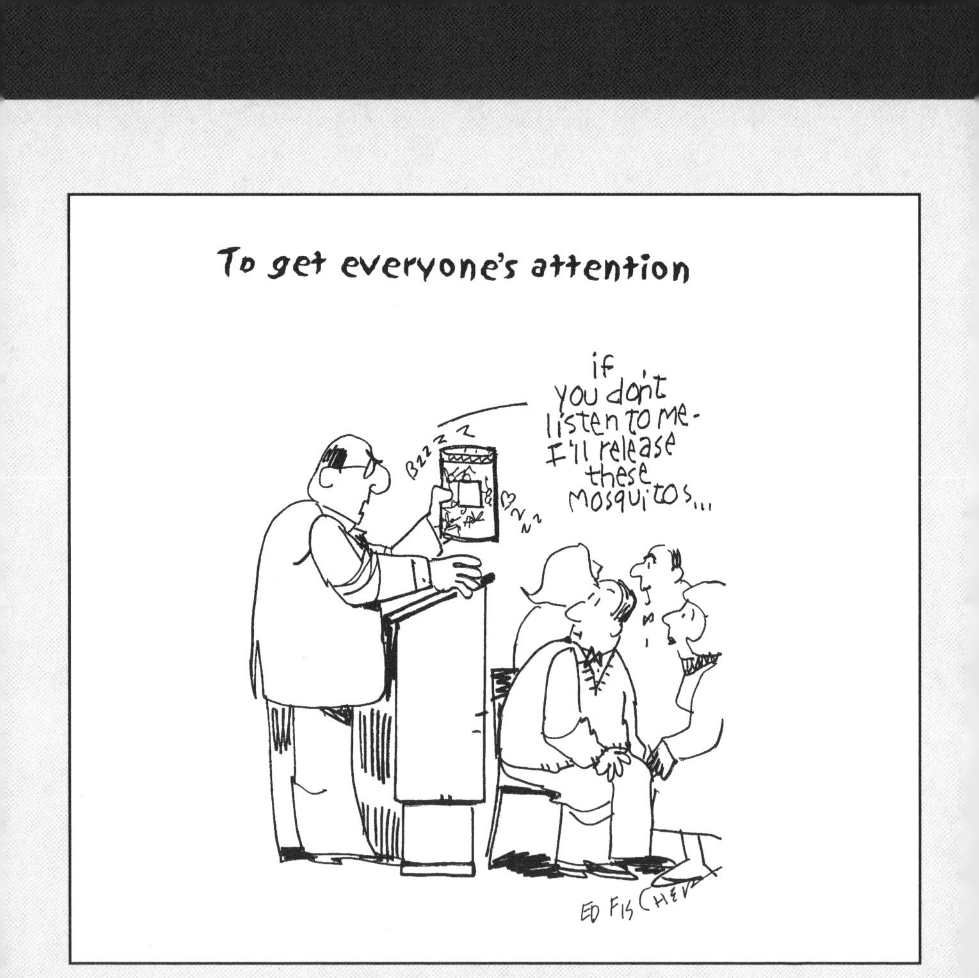
if you don't listen to me- I'll release these mosquitos...
BZZZZ
ED FISCHER

Bait (to catch suckers)

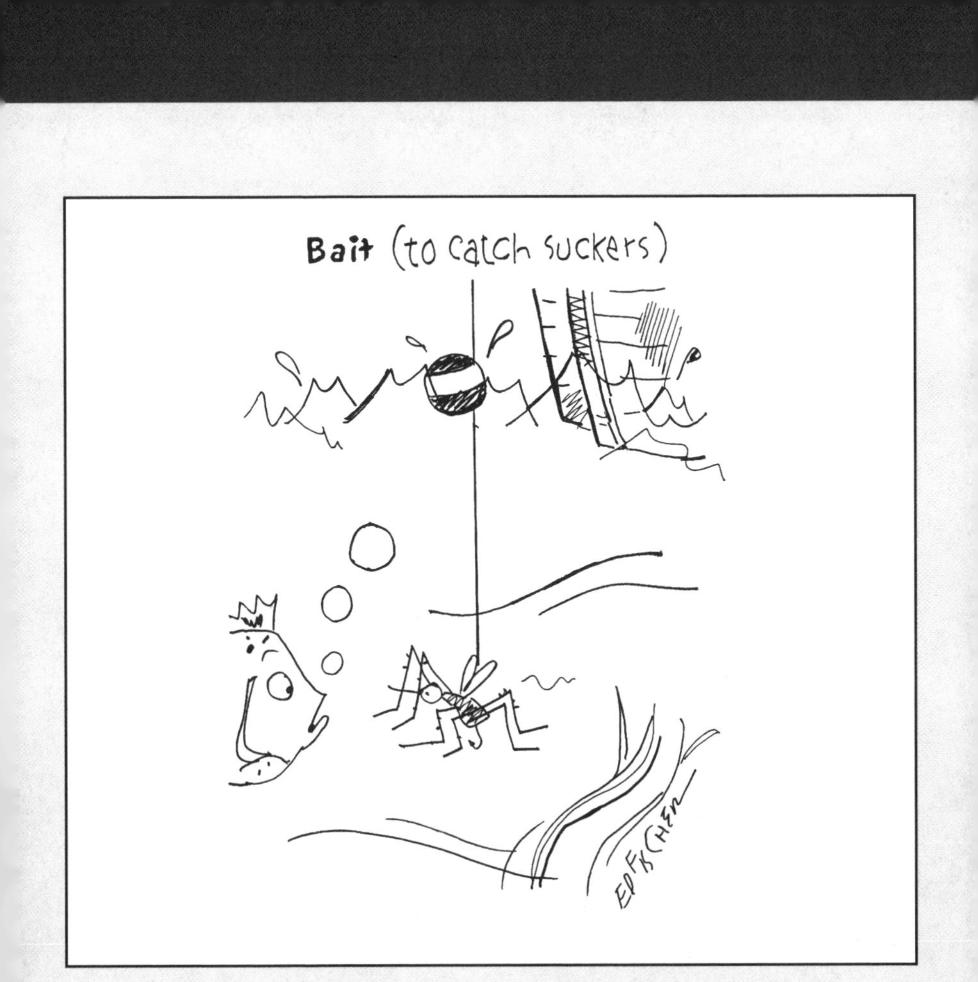

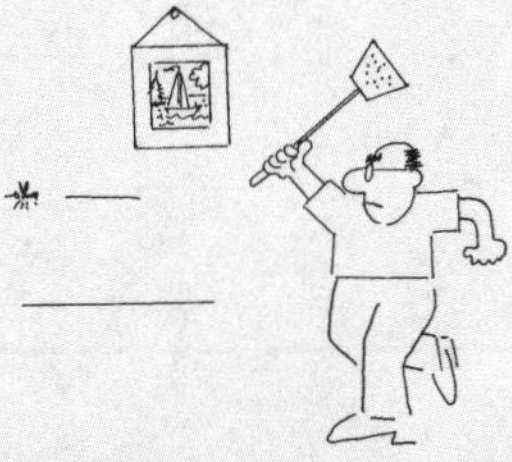

To clear a beach

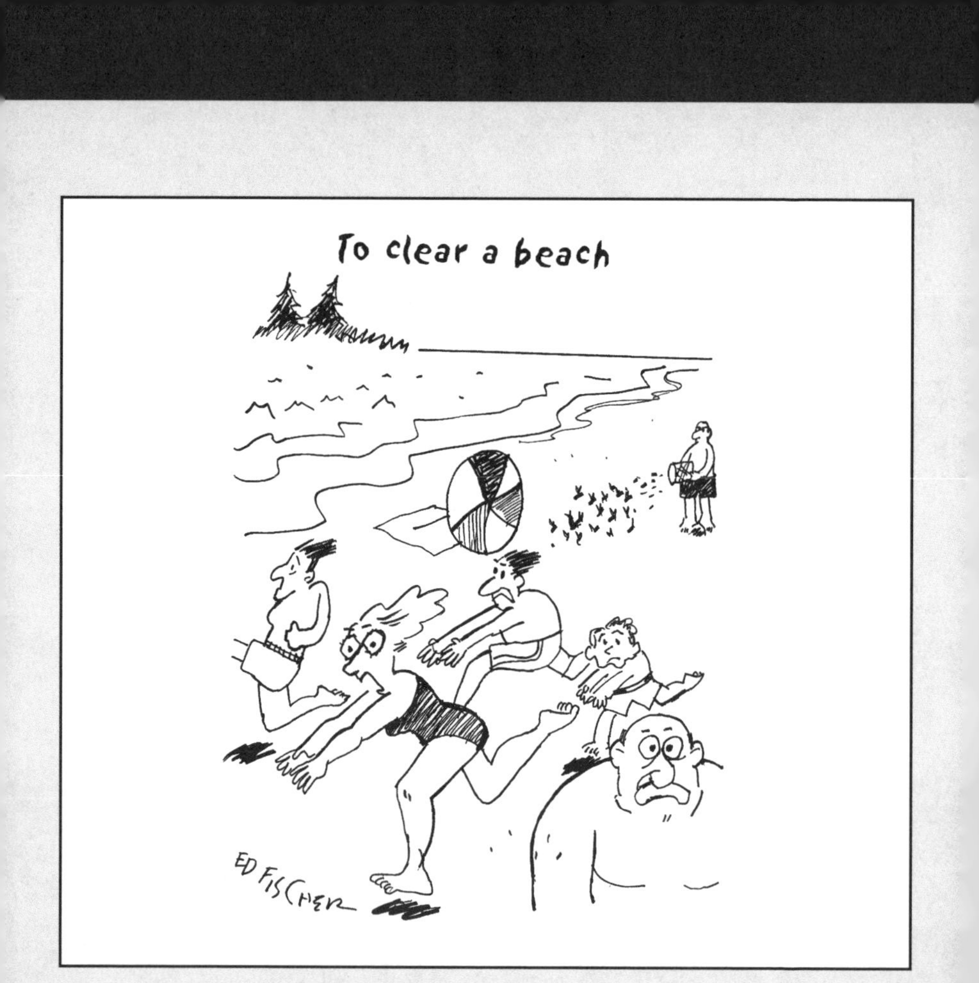
ED FISCHER

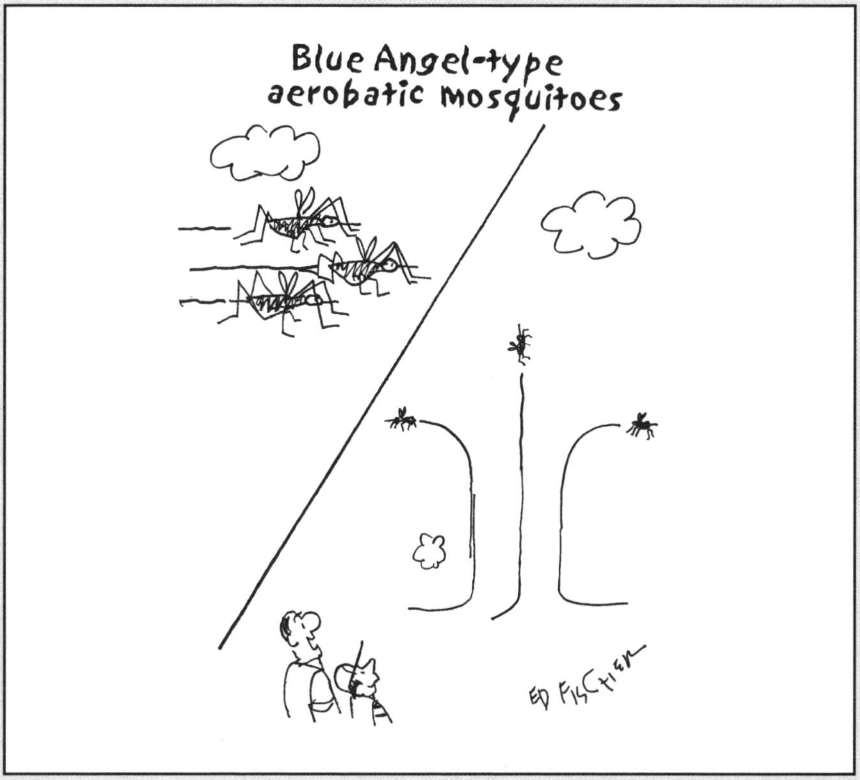
Blue Angel-type
aerobatic mosquitoes
ED FISCHER

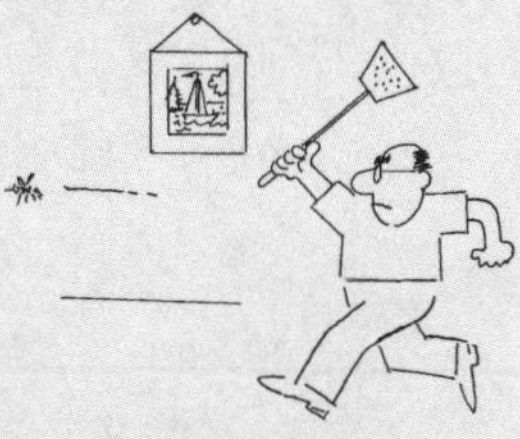

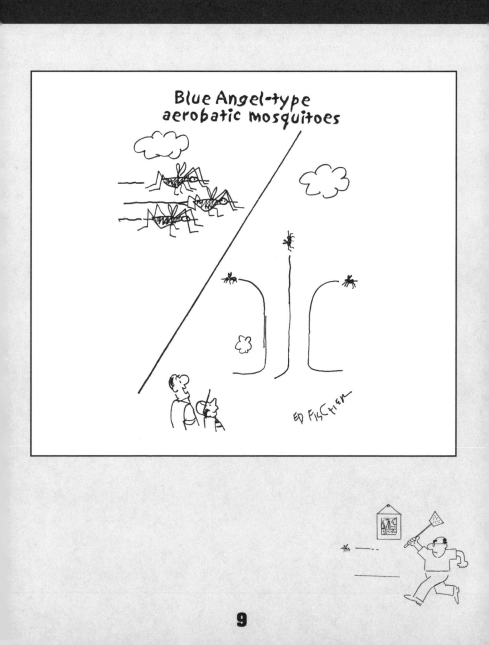

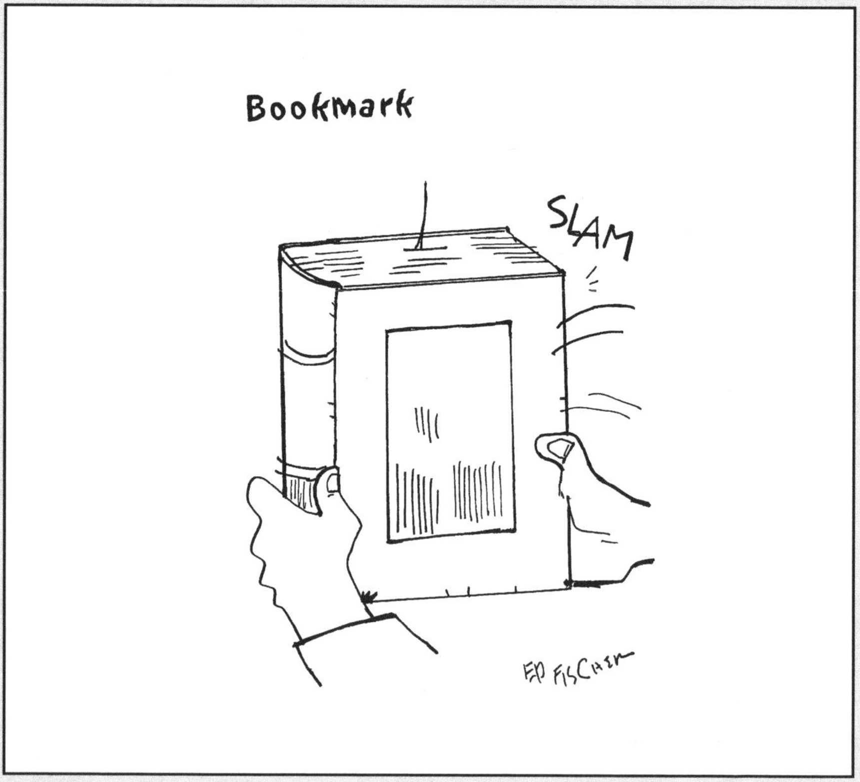
Bookmark
SLAM
ED FISCHER

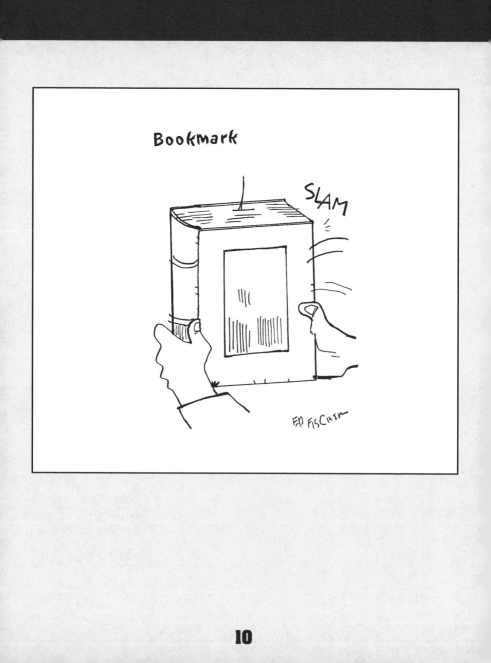

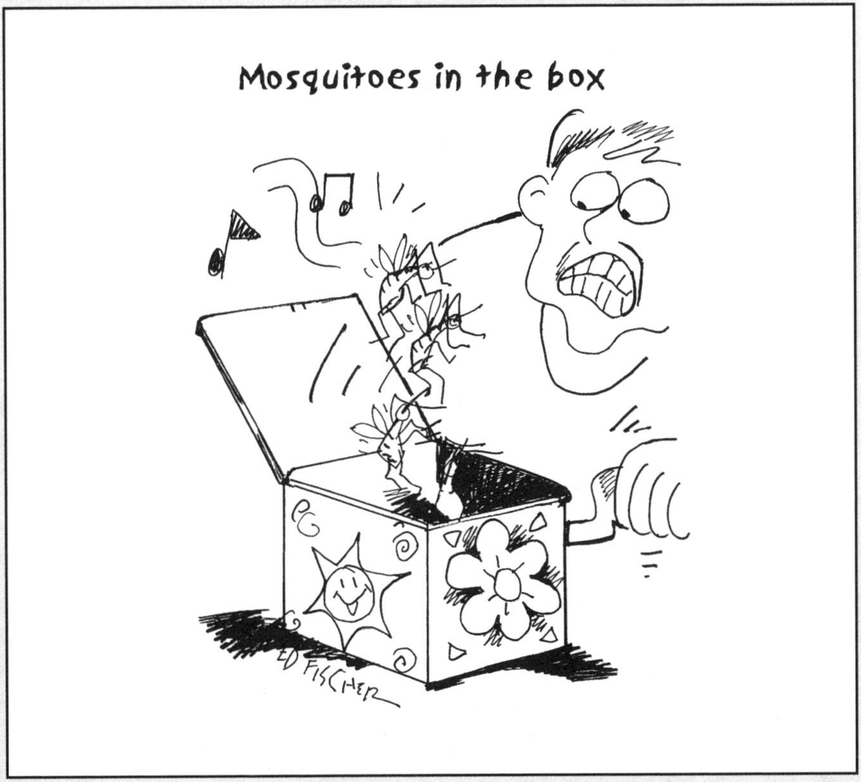
Mosquitoes in the box
ED FISCHER

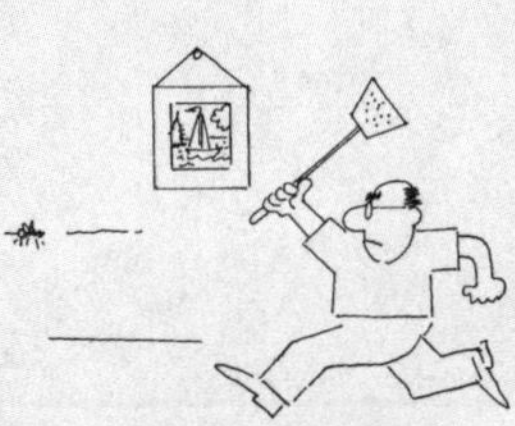

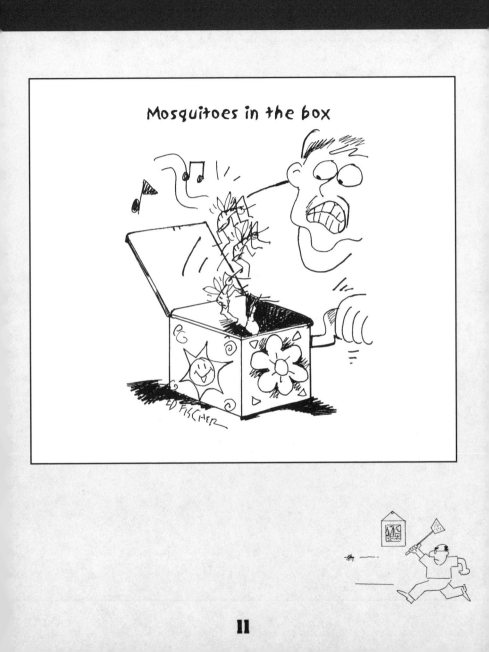

Try brainwashing

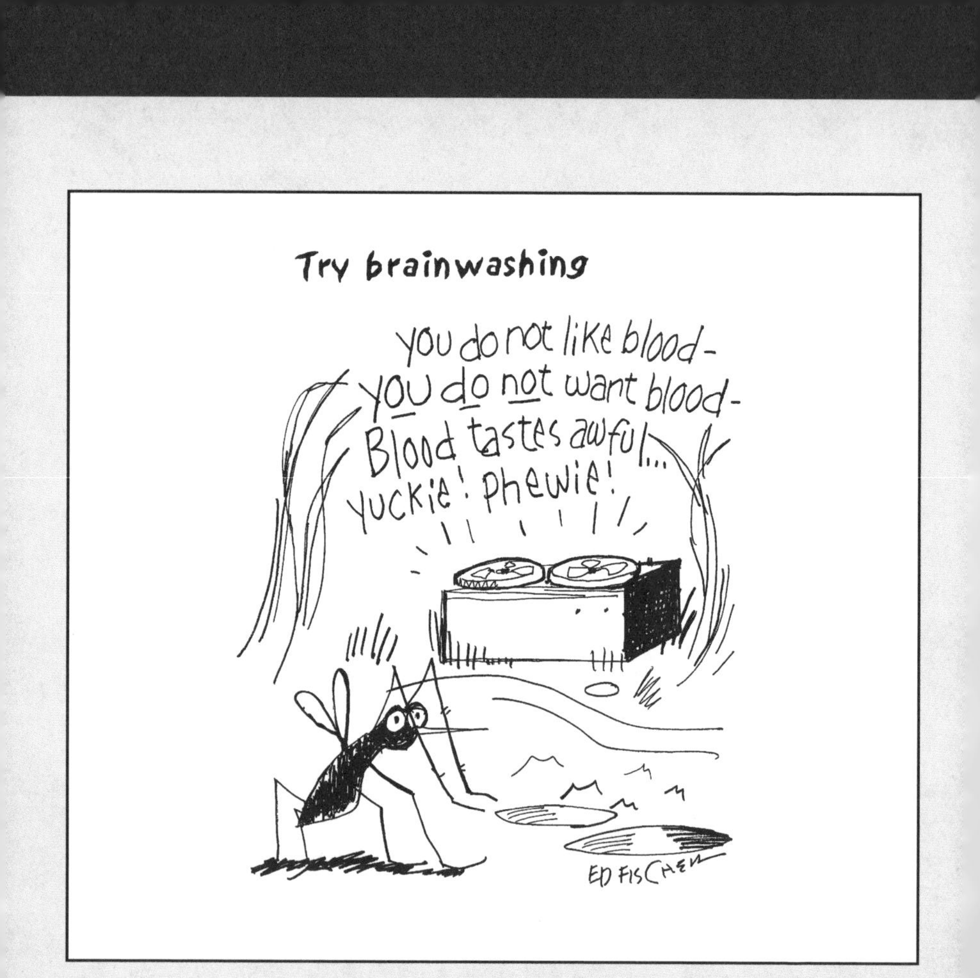
you do not like blood-
you do not want blood-
Blood tastes awful...
yuckie! phewie!
ED FISCHER

Start a BSA

Blood Suckers Anonymous
Hi- my name is Mildred and I'm a bloodoholic
Hi, Mildred
ED FISCHER

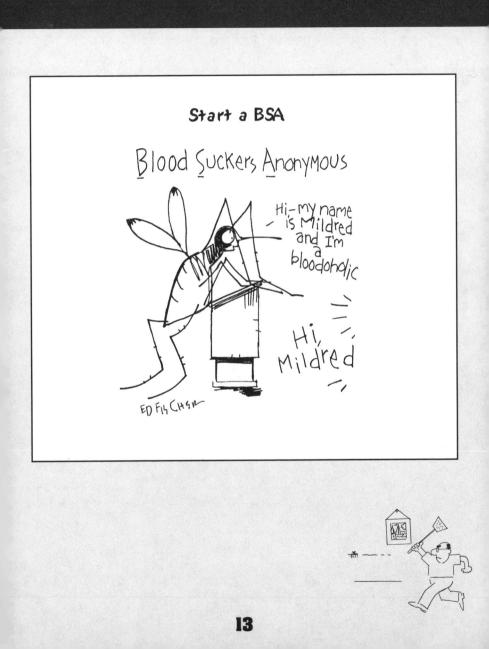

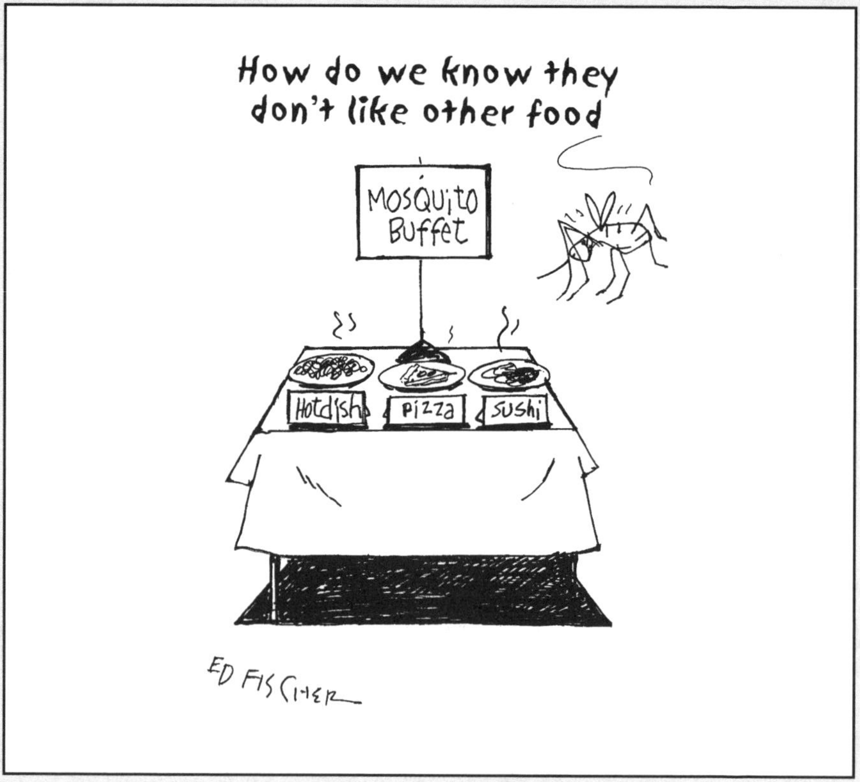
How do we know they don't like other food
MOSQUITO Buffet
Hotdish
pizza
sushi
ED FISCHER

To portage canoes

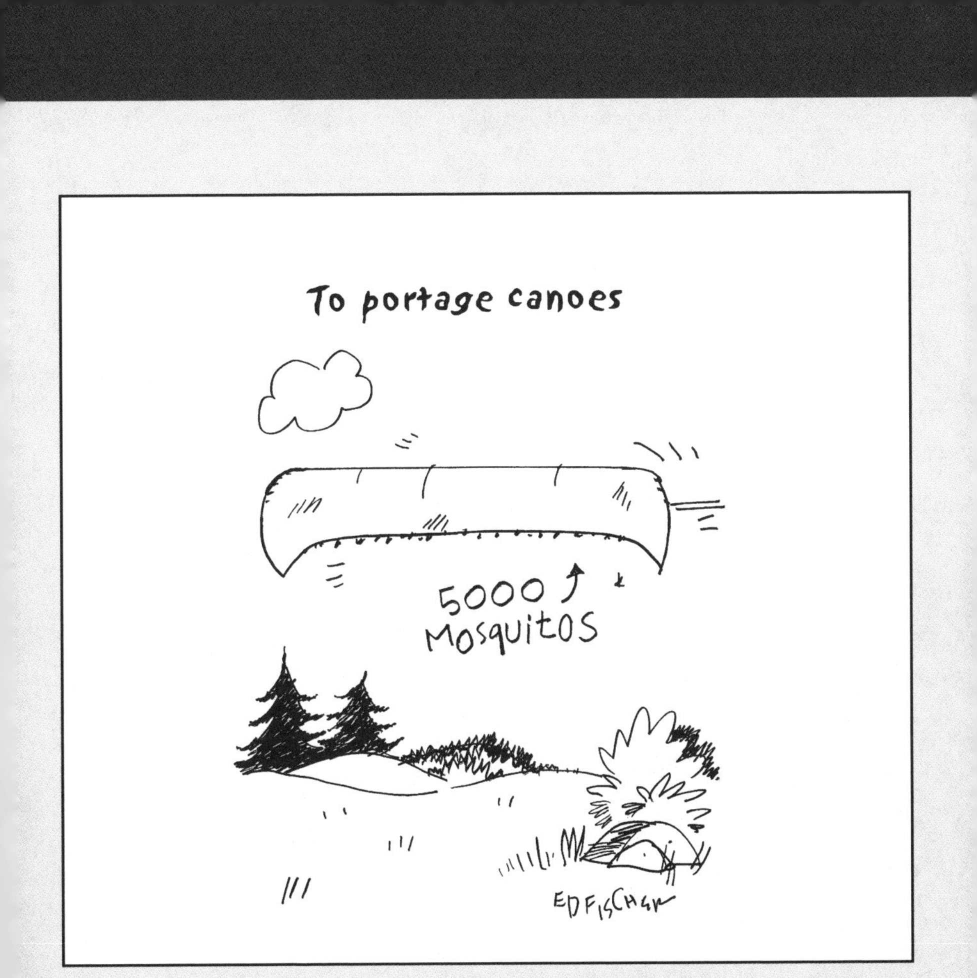
5000
Mosquitos
EDFISCHER

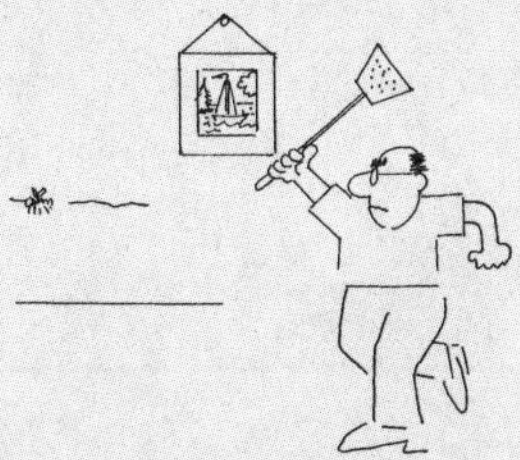

To prevent carjackings

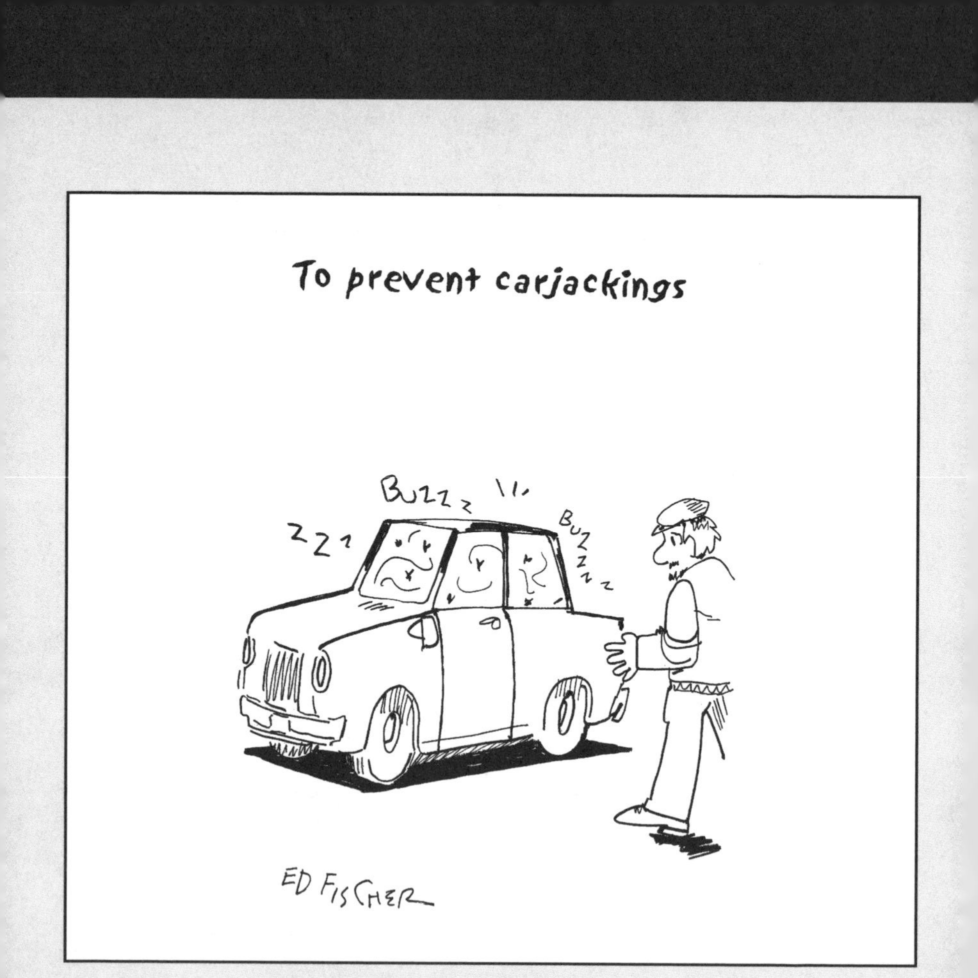
BUZZZZ
ZZZ
ED FISCHER

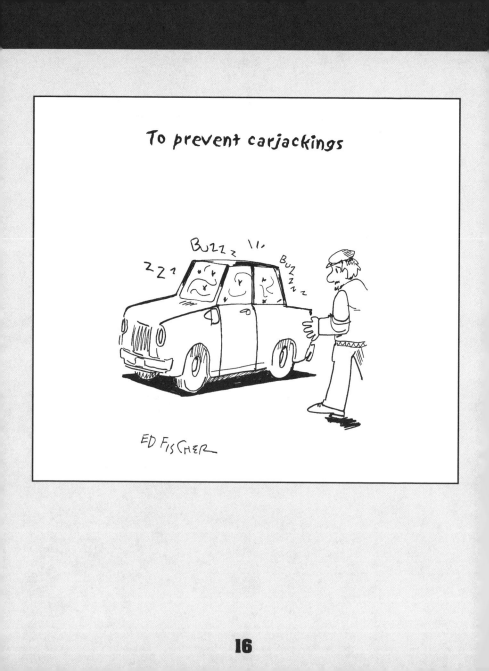

Train carrier mosquitoes
to deliver small messages

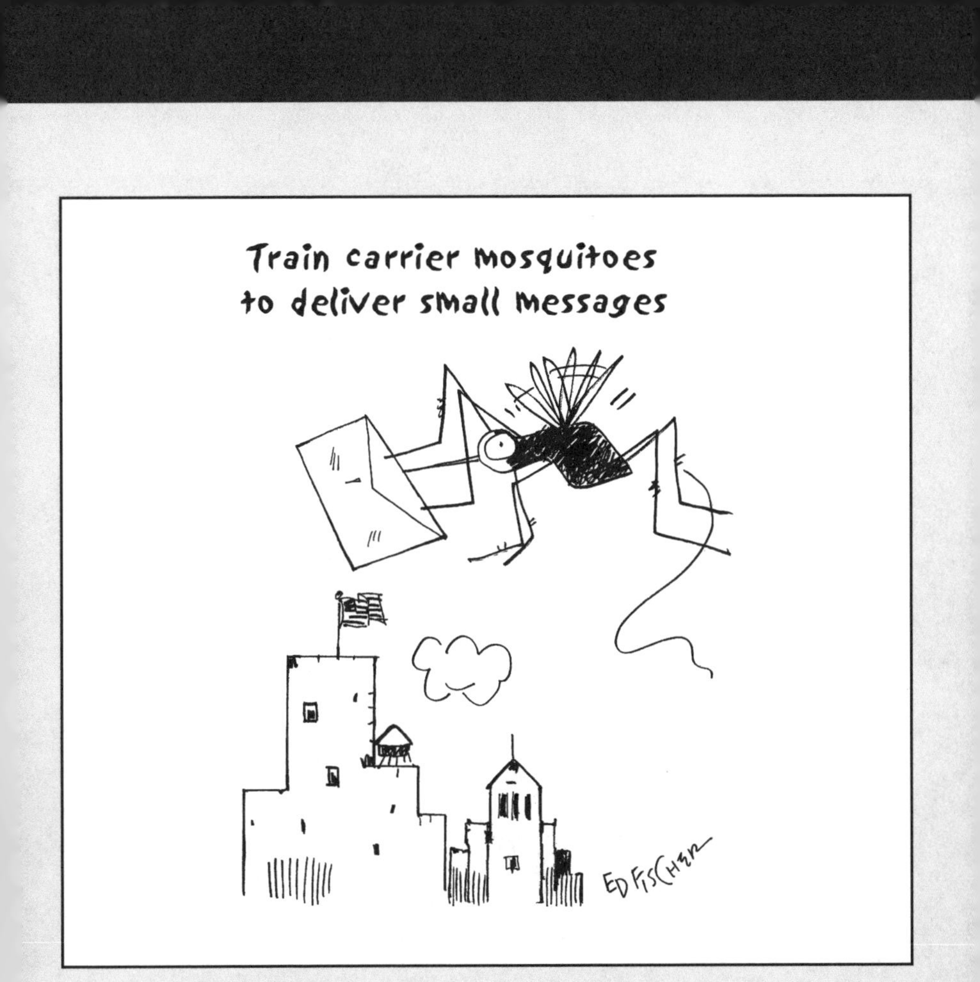
ED FISCHER

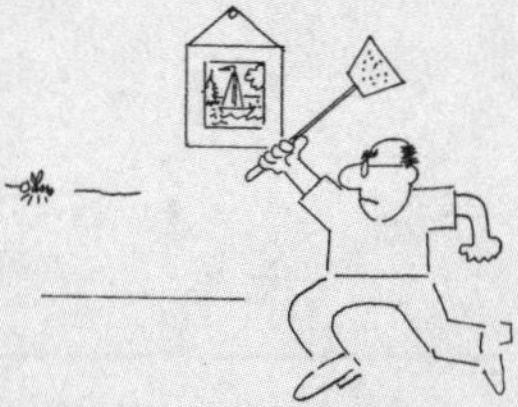

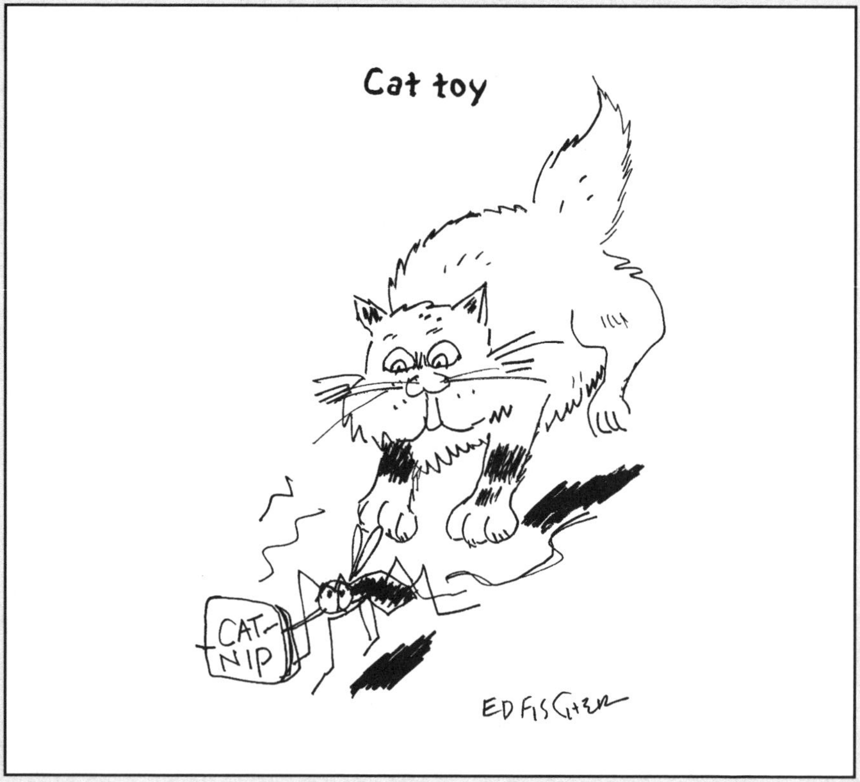
Cat toy
CAT-
NIP
EDFISCHER

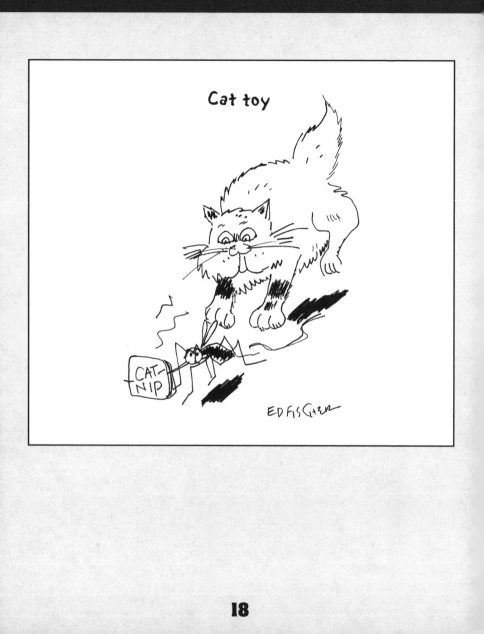

To make chess tournaments more interesting

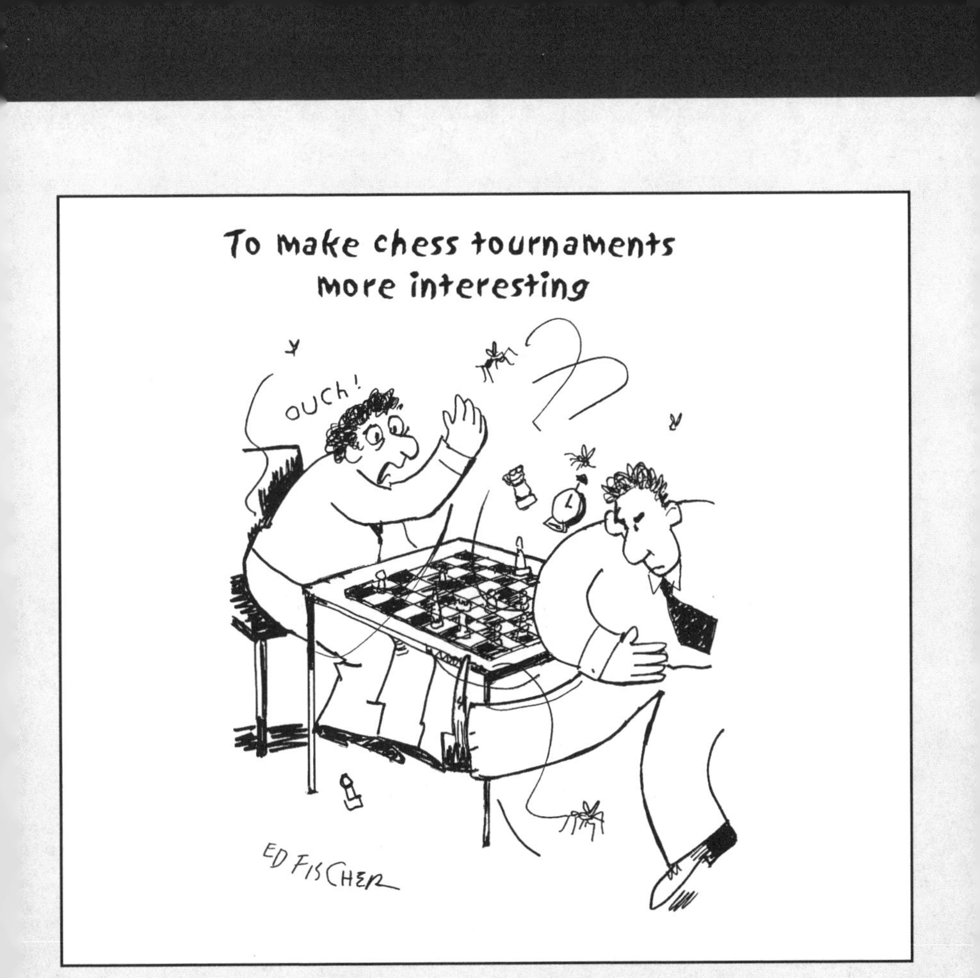
OUCH!
ED FISCHER

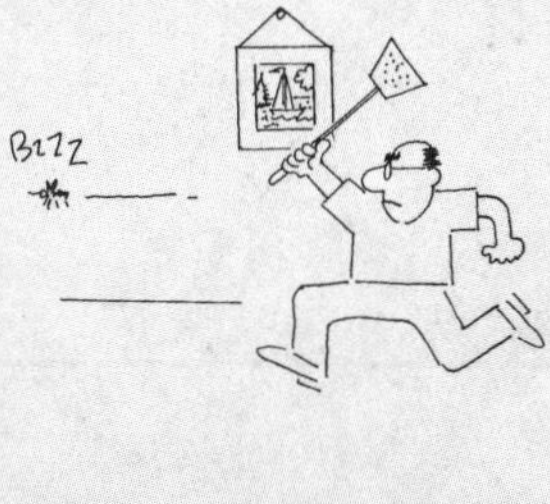
BZZZ

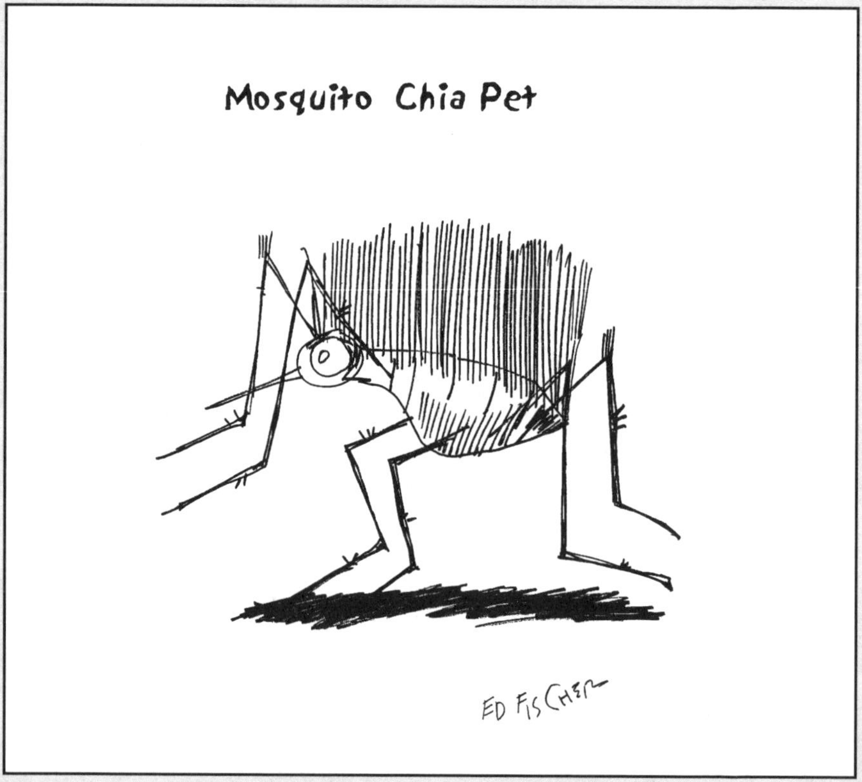
Mosquito Chia Pet
ED FISCHER

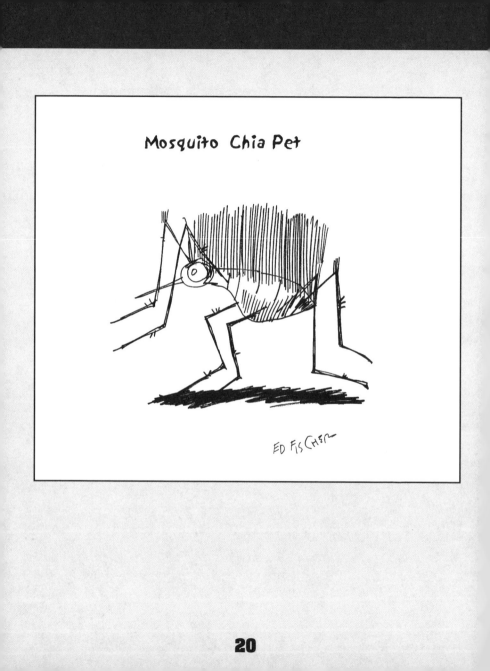

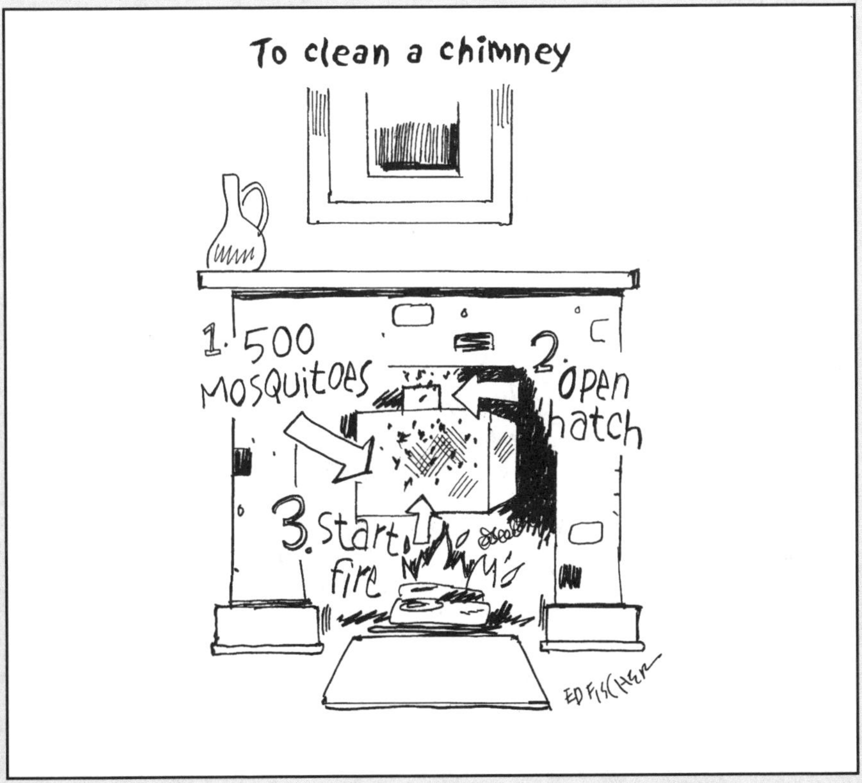
To clean a chimney
1. 500 MOSQUITOES
2. open hatch
3. start fire
ED FISCHER

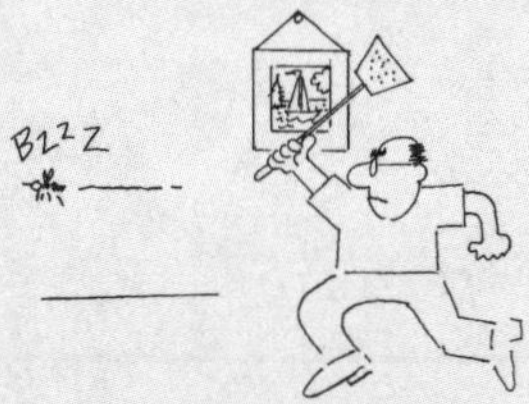
BZZZ

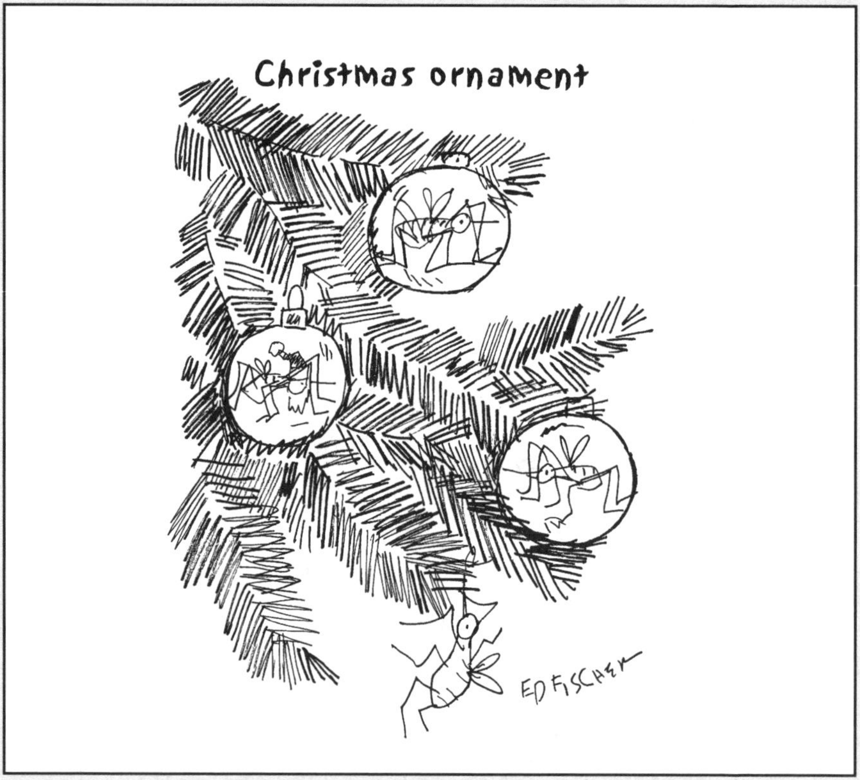
Christmas ornament
ED FISCHER

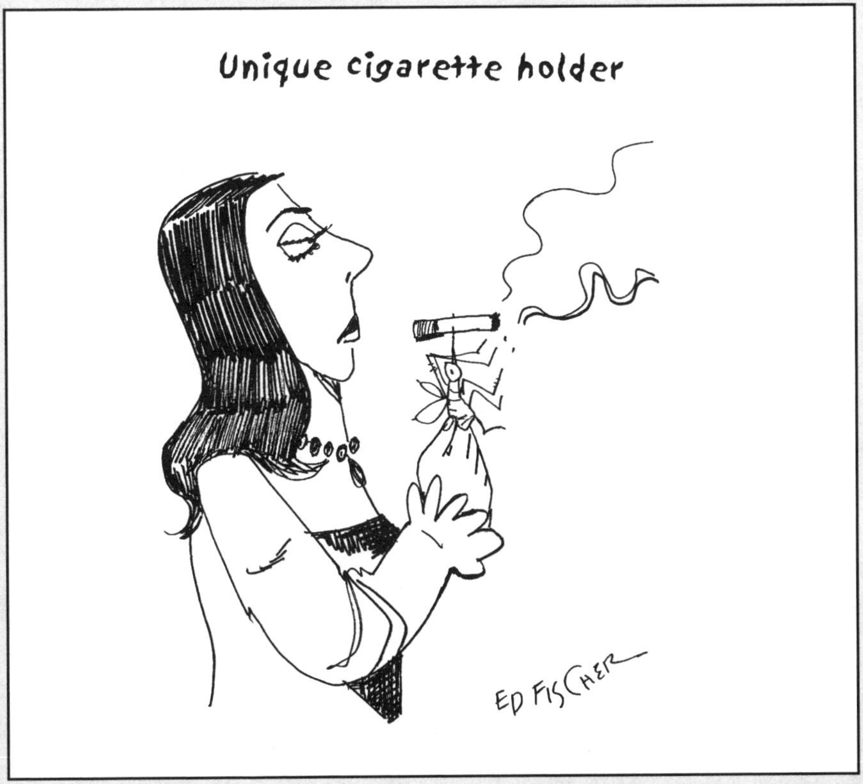
Unique cigarette holder
ED FISCHER

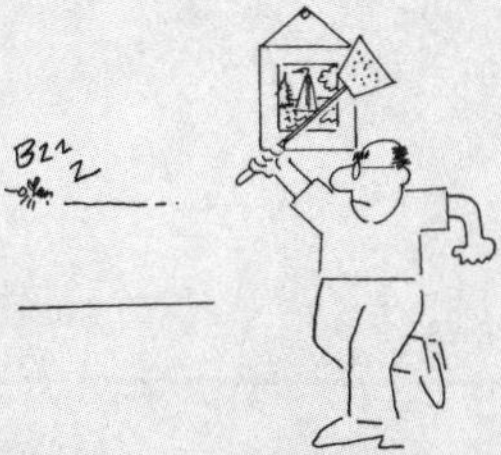
BZZ Z

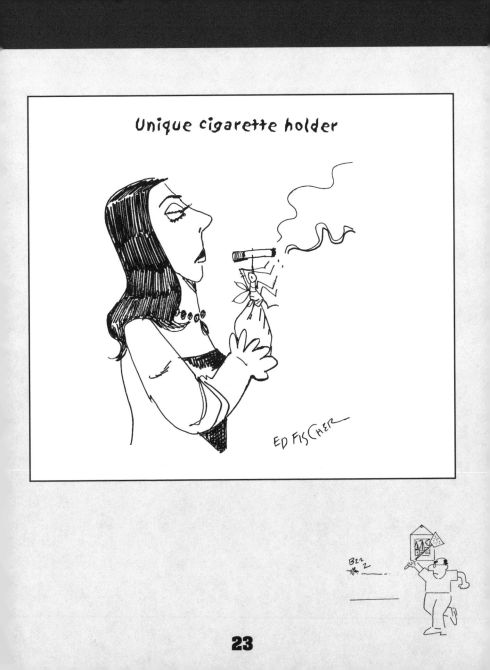

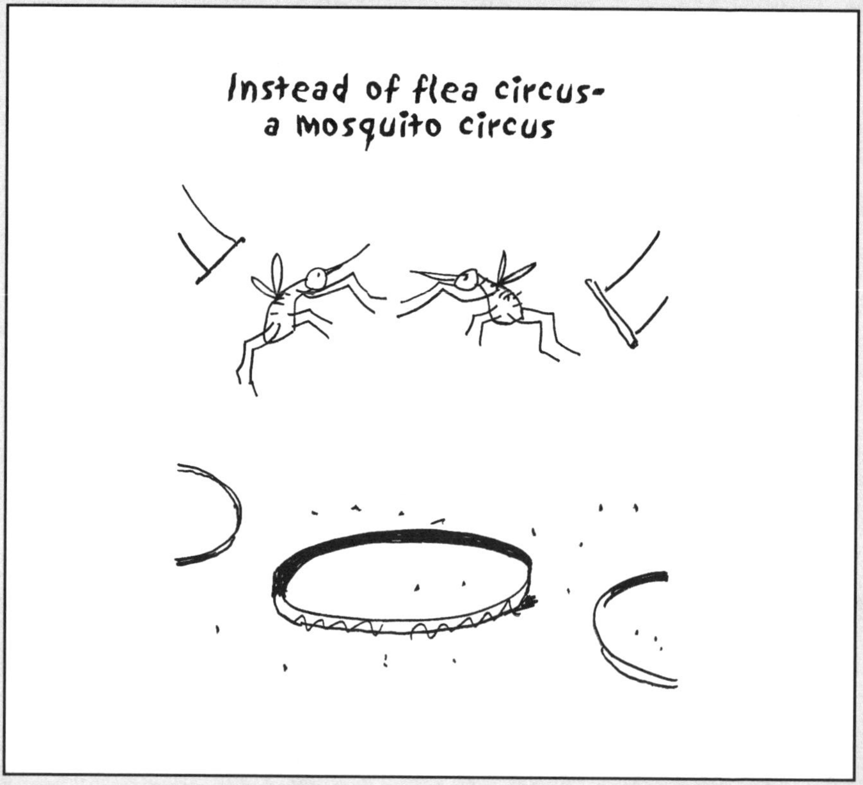
Instead of flea circus-
a mosquito circus

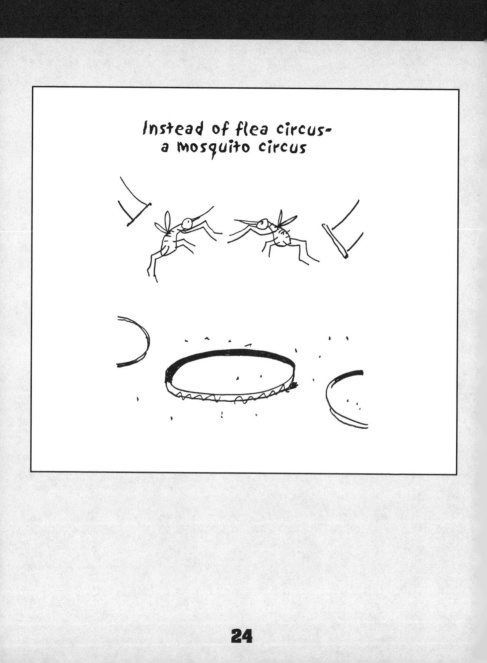

For something kind of funny-
to hold up a clown's pants

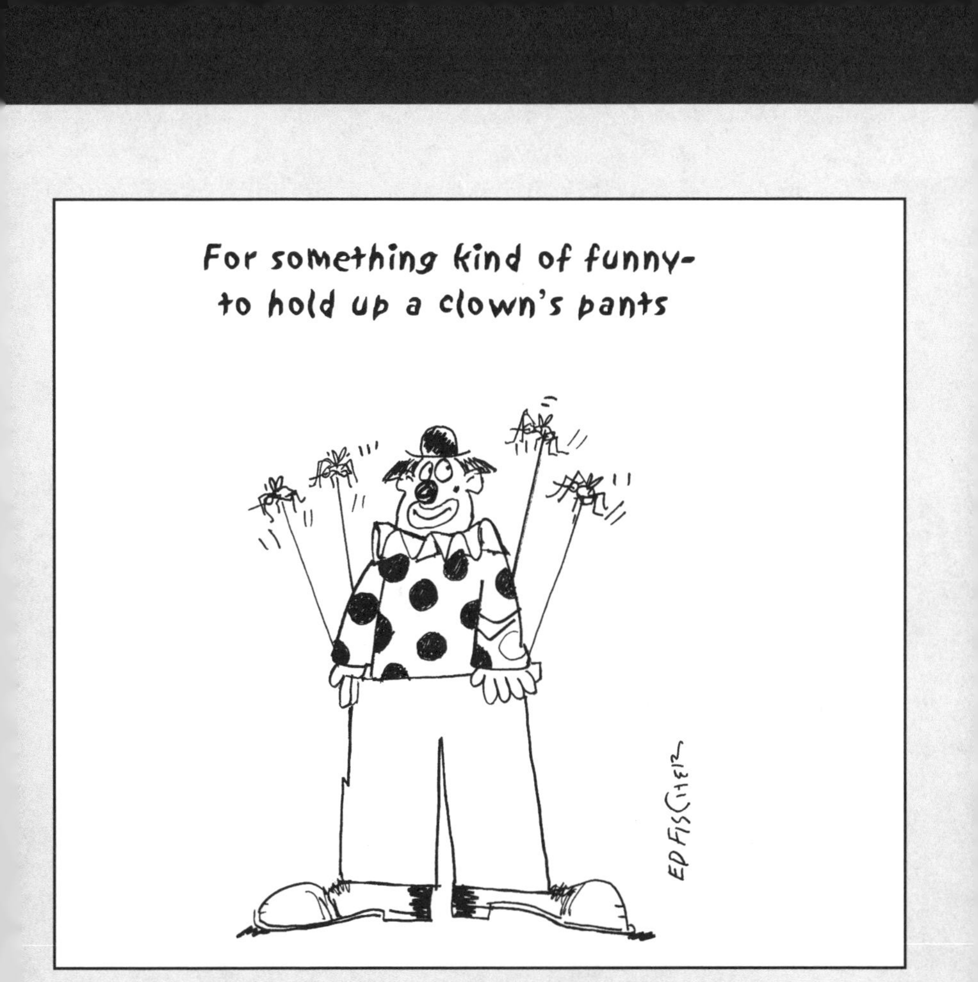
ED FISCHER

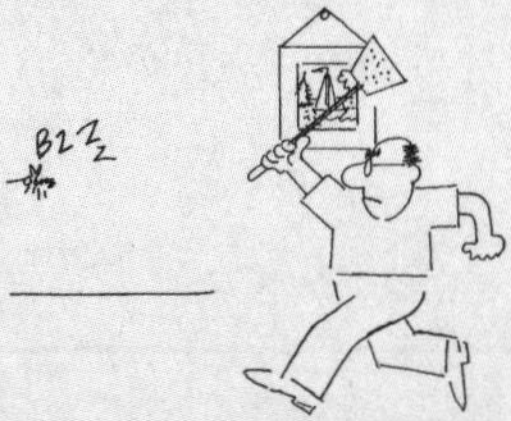
BZZZ

Get them hyped up on coffee

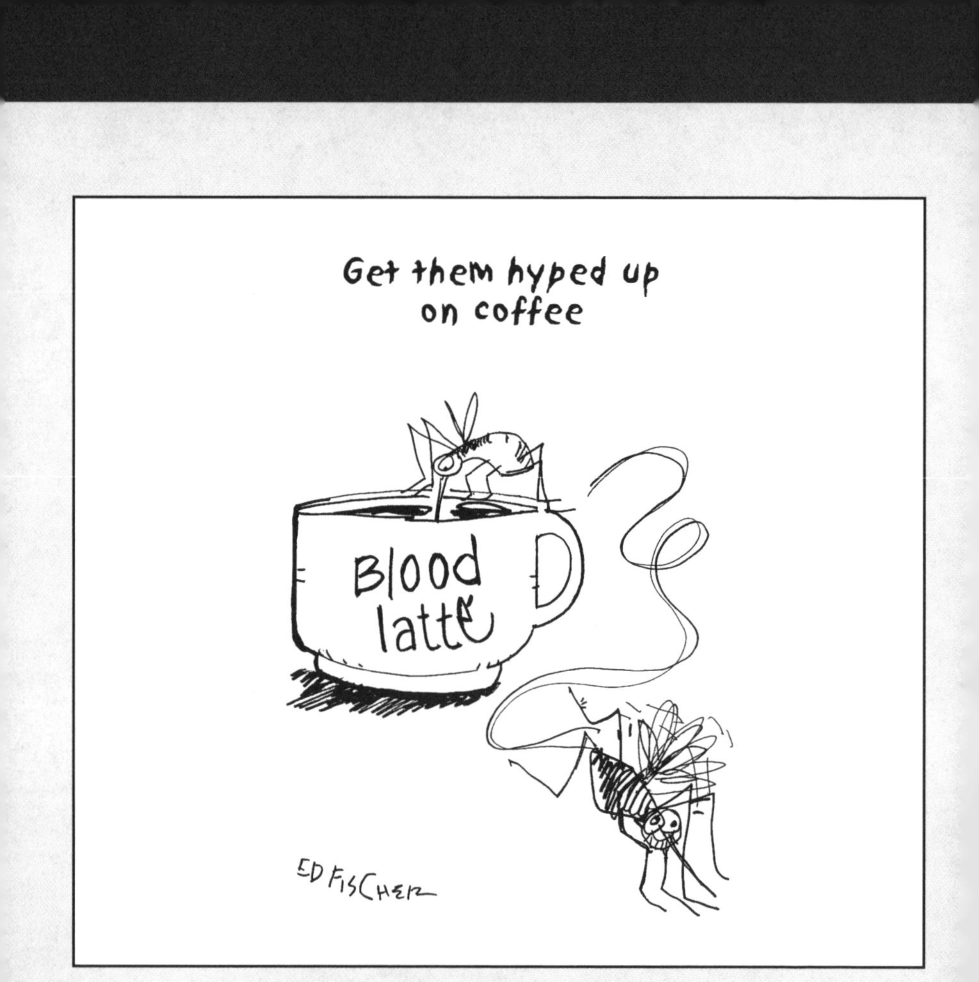
Blood latte
ED FISCHER

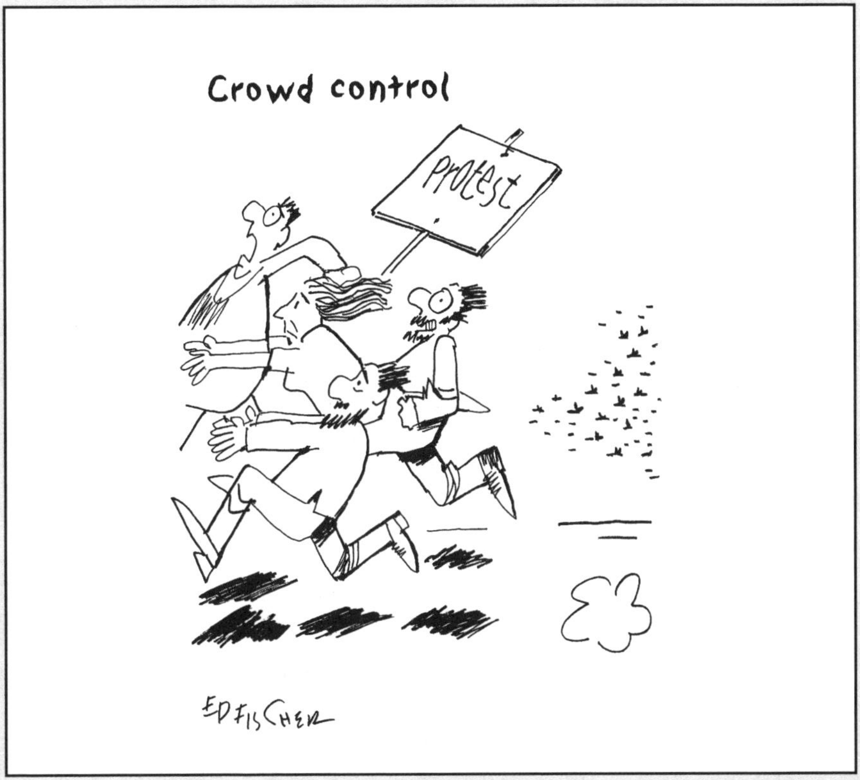
Crowd control
Protest
ED FISCHER

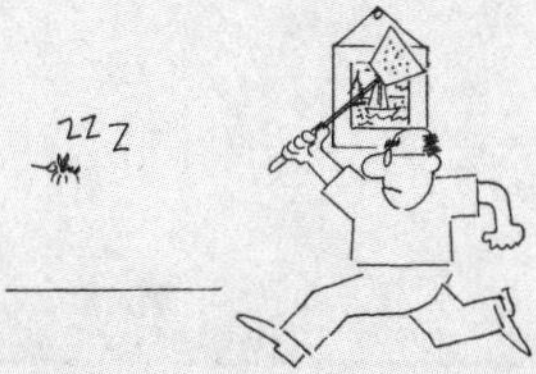
ZZZ

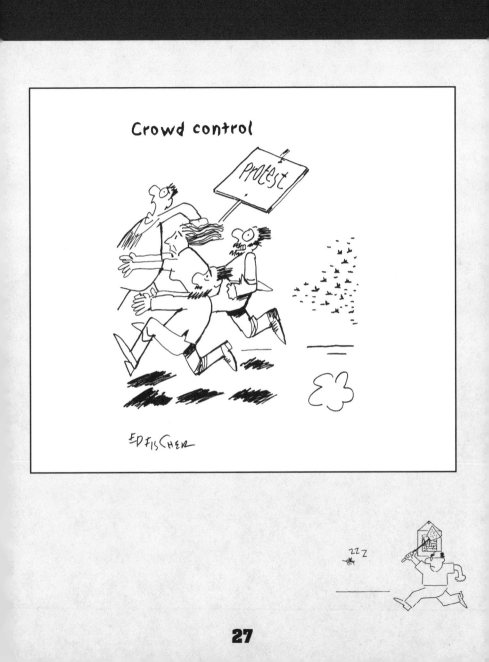

To tell you when you're too close to the curb

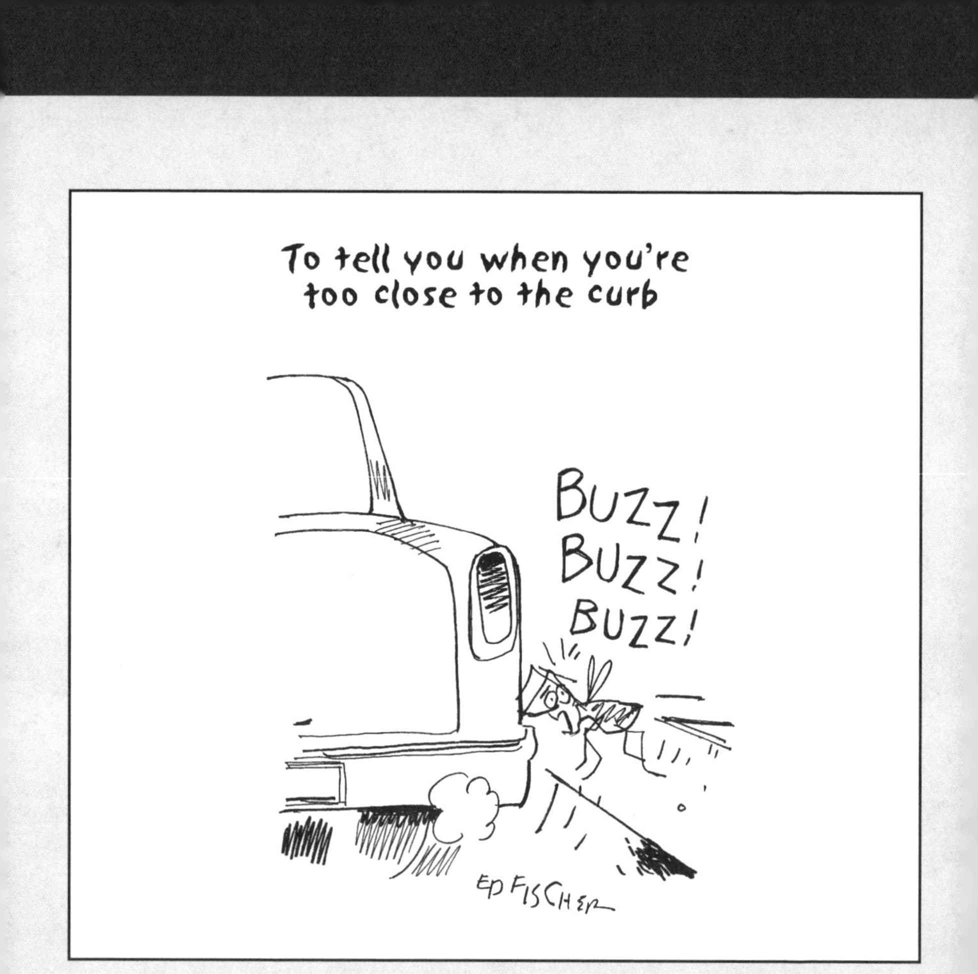
BUZZ!
BUZZ!
BUZZ!
ED FISCHER

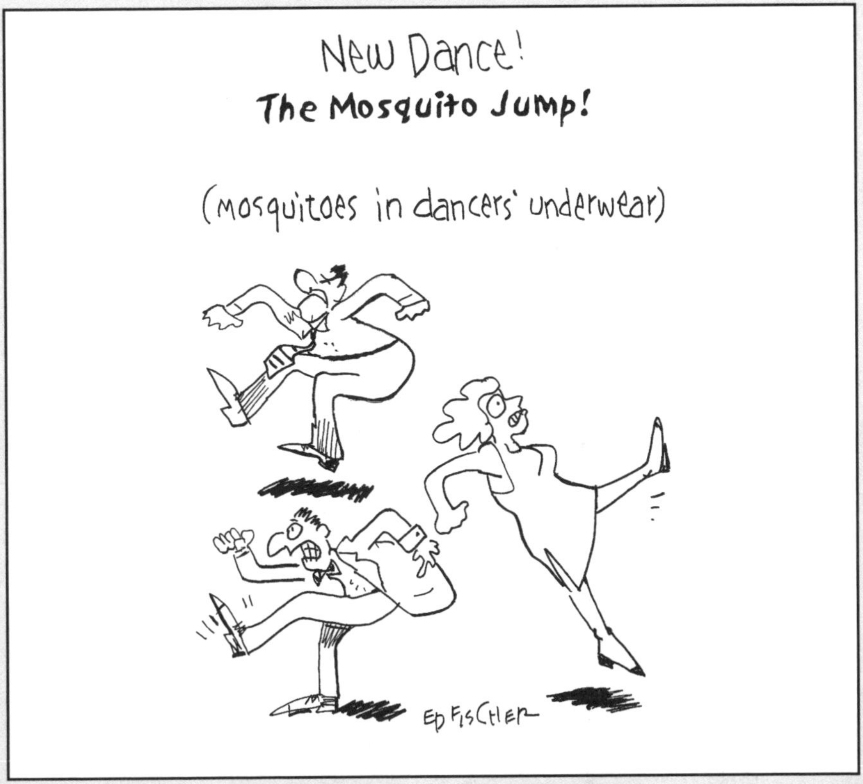
New Dance!
The Mosquito Jump!
(mosquitoes in dancers' underwear)
ED FISCHER

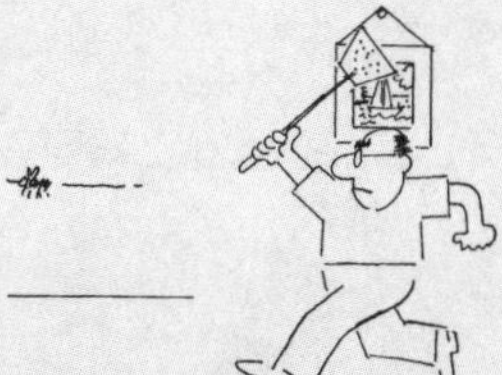

To give you an edge at a dart tournament

Buzzz...
Plunk
Ed Fischer

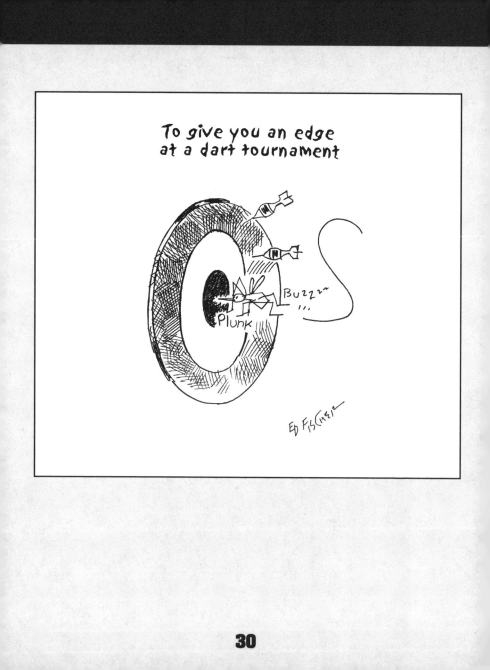

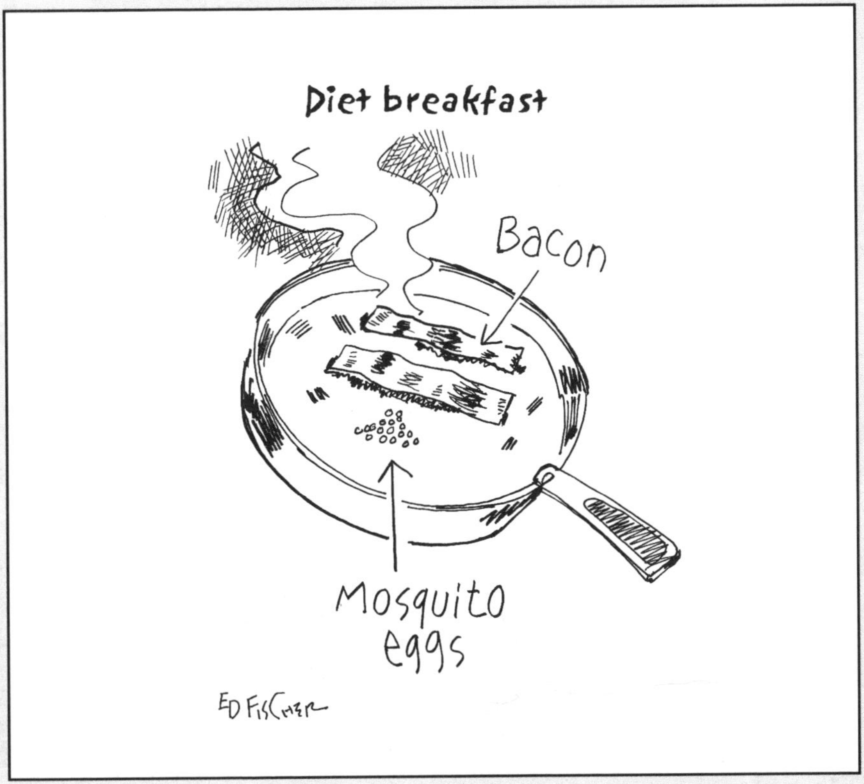
Diet breakfast
Bacon
Mosquito eggs
ED FISCHER

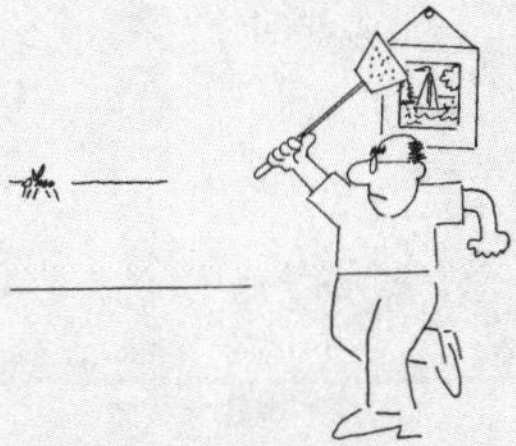

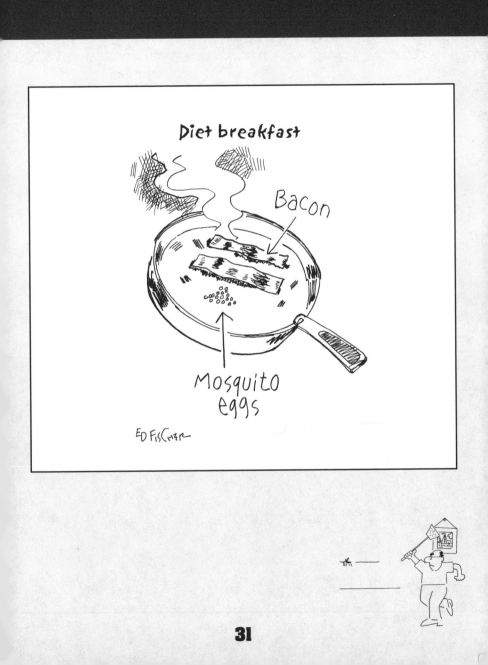

Marketing possibilities

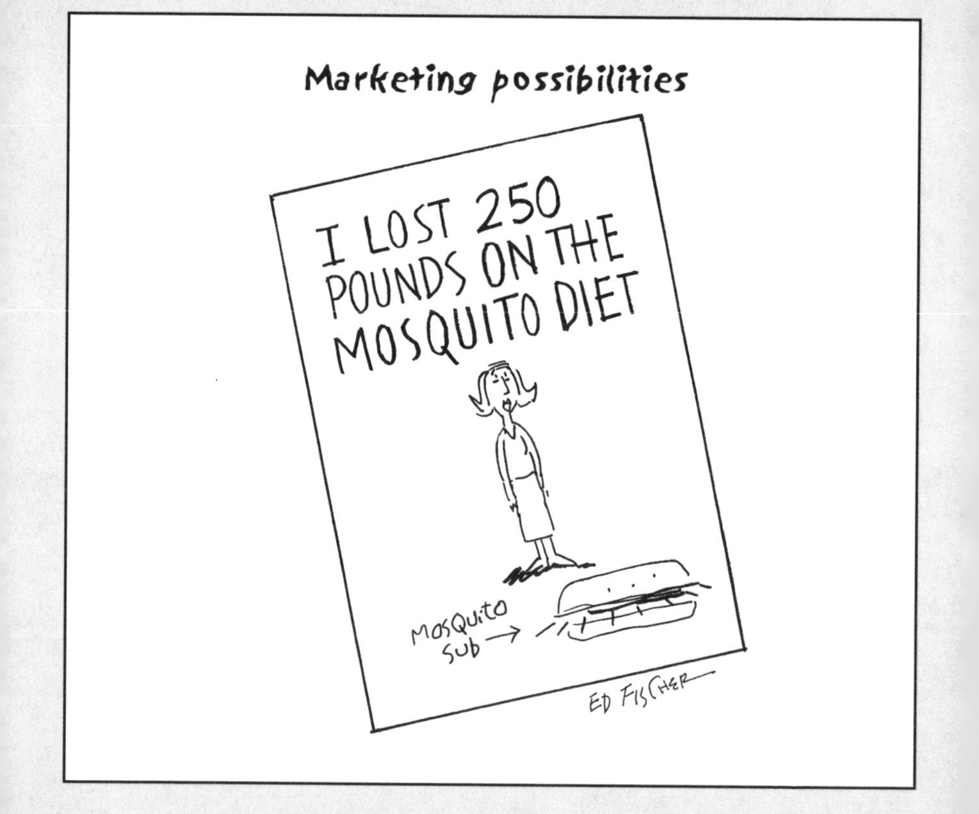
I LOST 250
POUNDS ON THE
MOSQUITO DIET
MOSQUITO
SUB
ED FISCHER

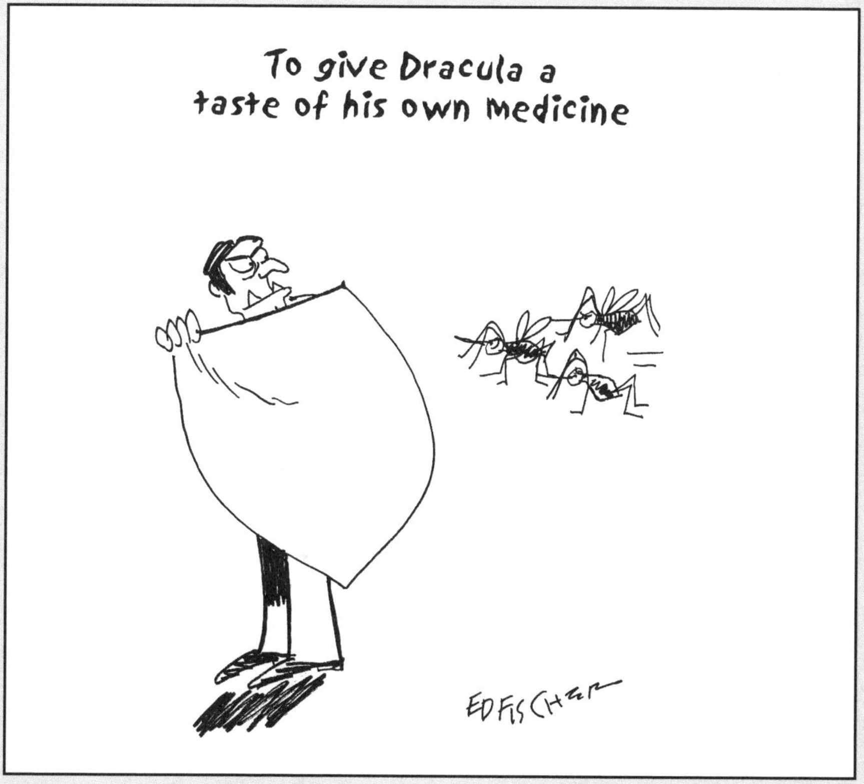
ED FISCHER

To give Dracula a
taste of his own medicine

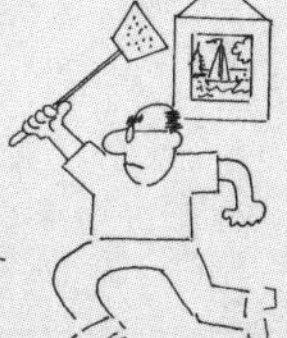

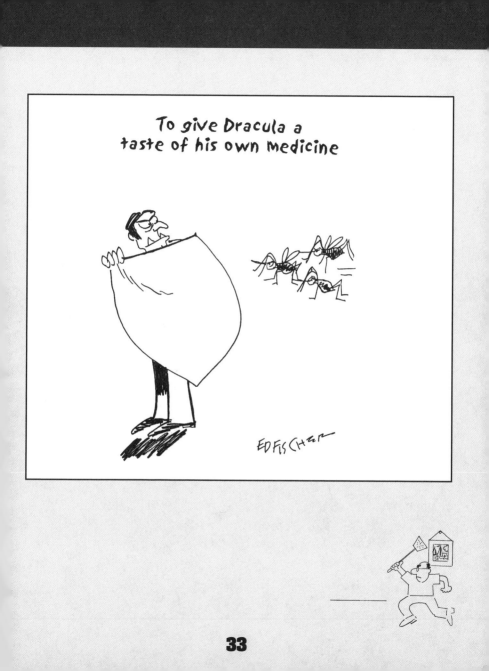

Cross mosquito with duck
(better to hear them coming)

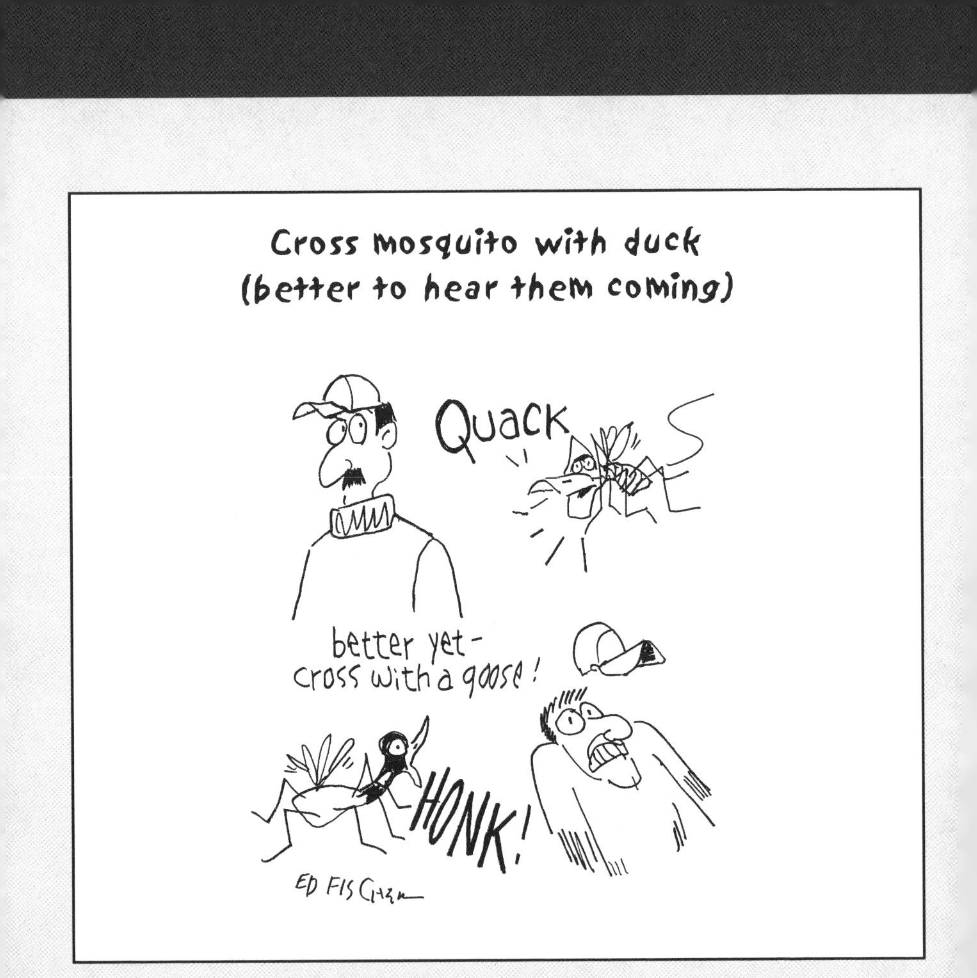
Quack
better yet -
cross with a goose!
HONK!

Earrings

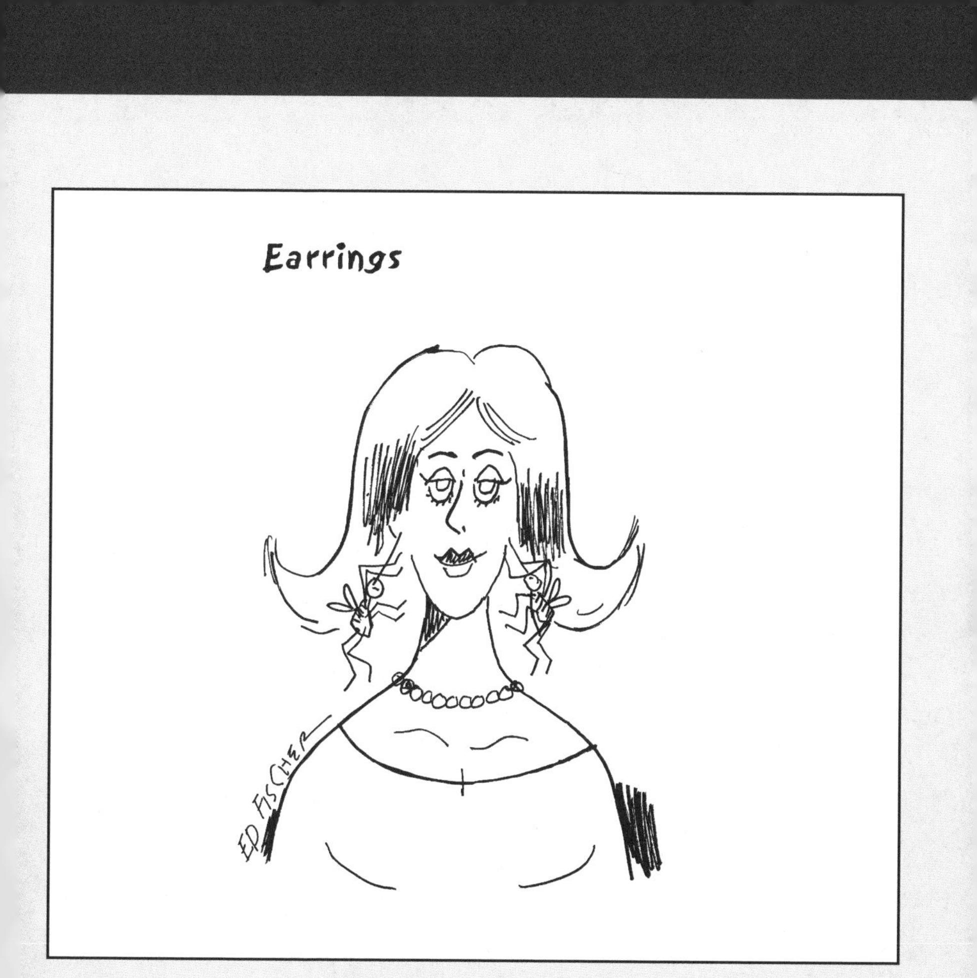
ED FISCHER

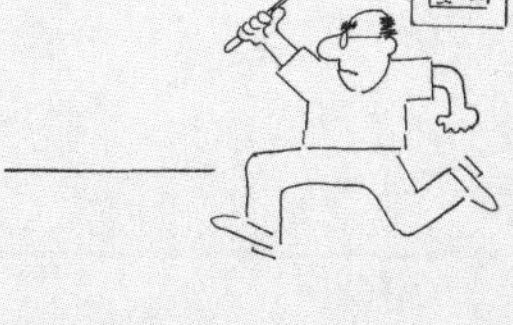

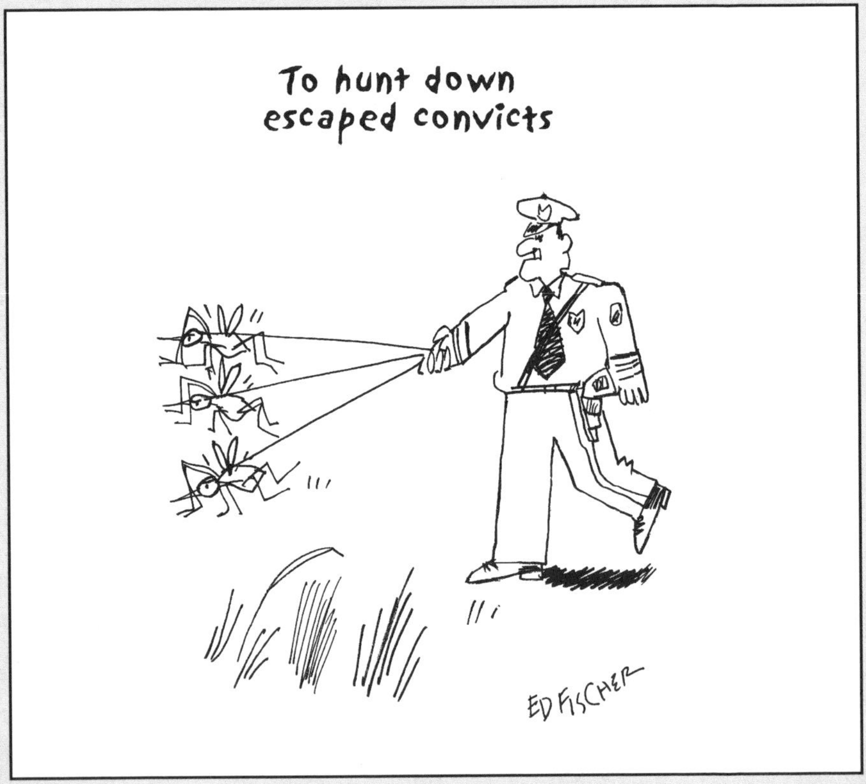
ED FISCHER

To hunt down escaped convicts

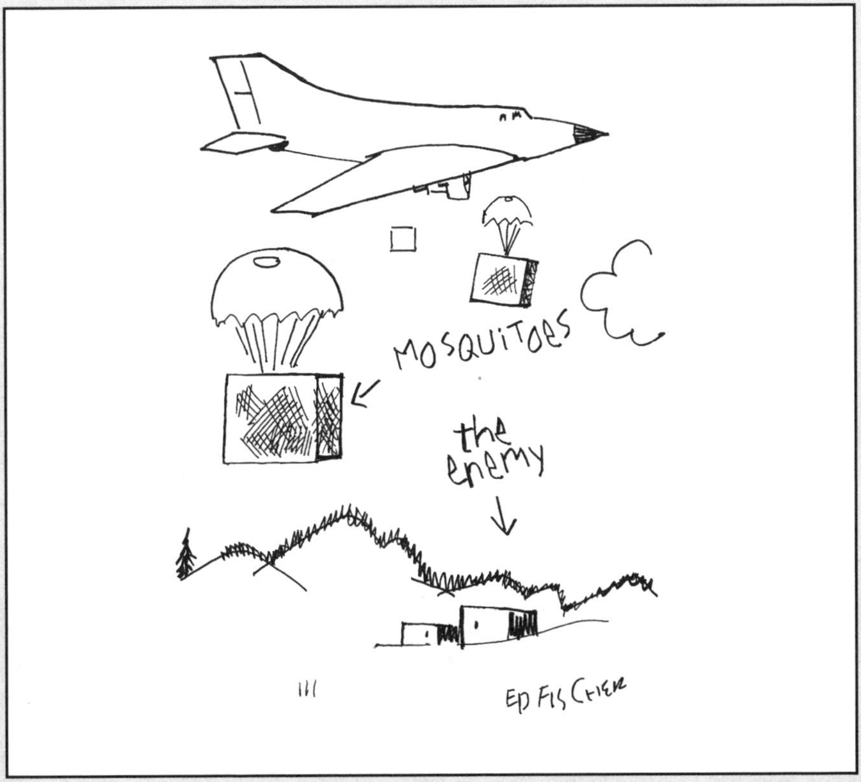
MOSQUITOES
the enemy
ED FISCHER

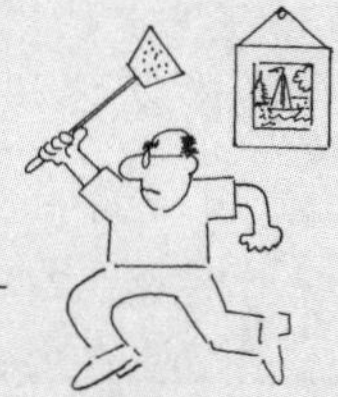

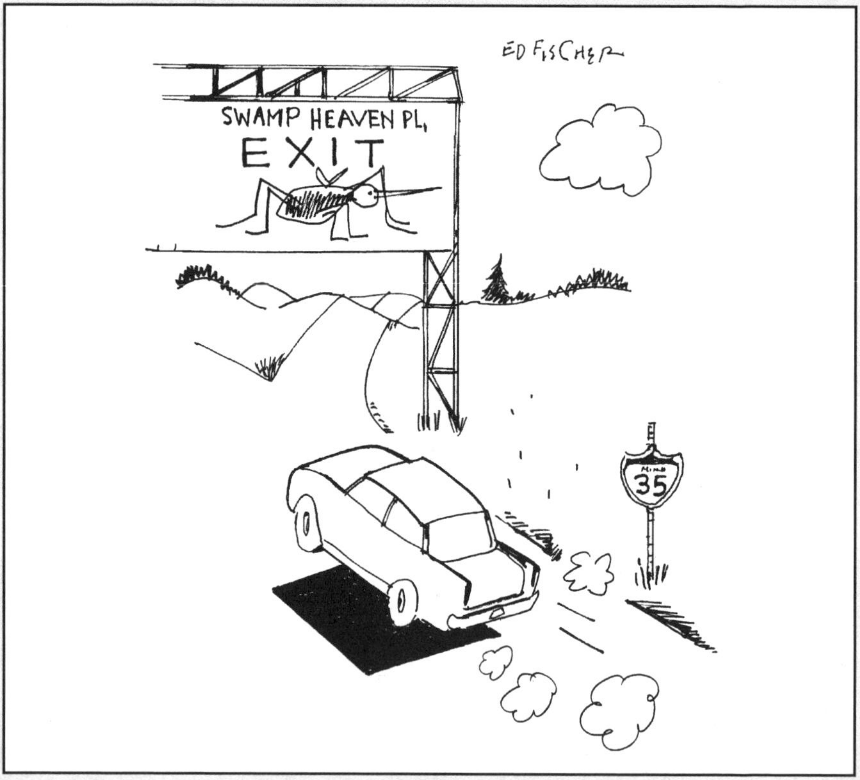
ED FISCHER
SWAMP HEAVEN PL.
EXIT
35

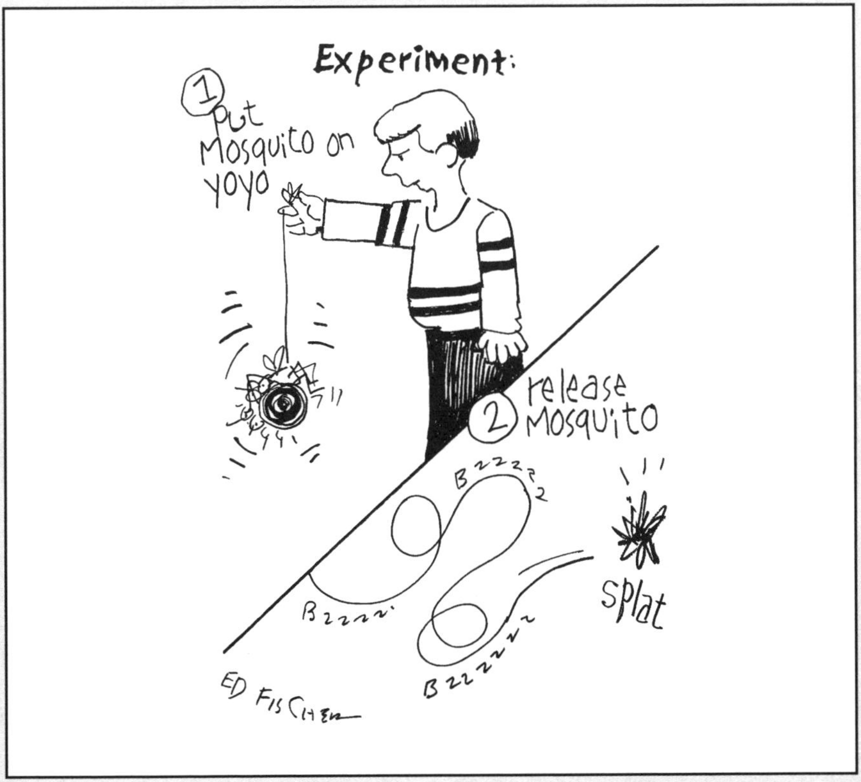
Experiment:
1 Put Mosquito on yoyo
2 release Mosquito
Bzzzzzz
Bzzzzz
Bzzzzzzz
Splat
ED FISCHER

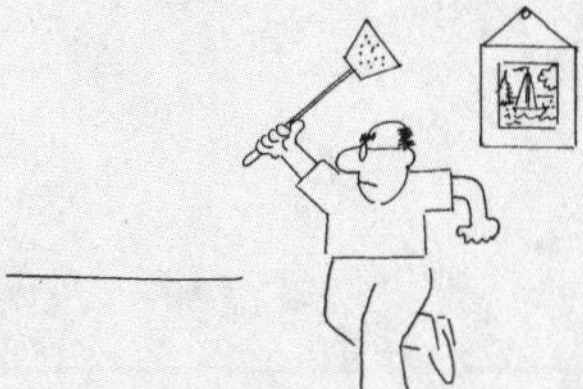

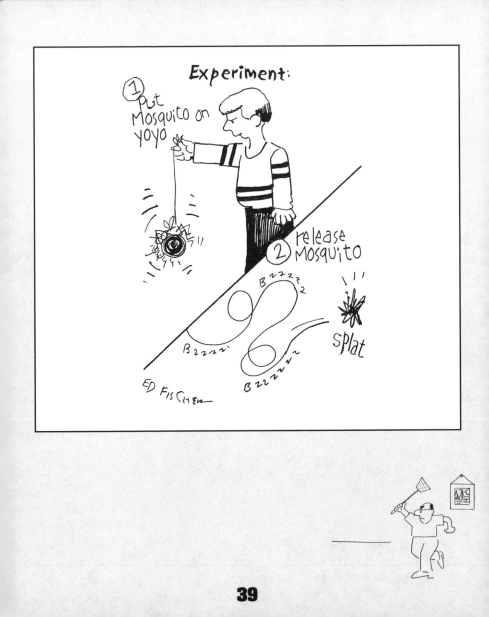

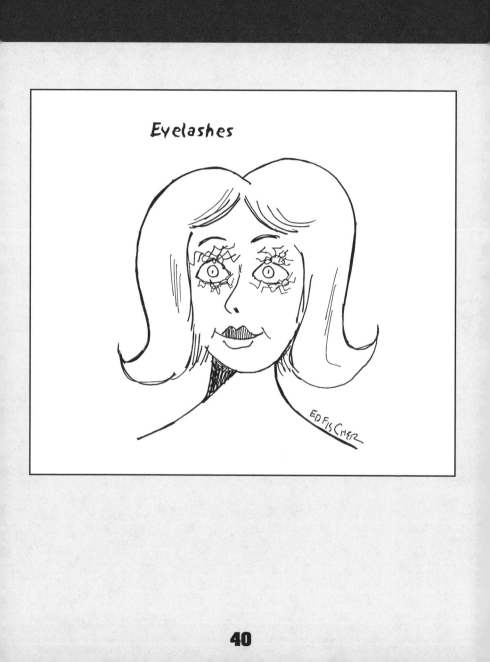

Eyelashes

ED FISCHER

Develop mosquitoes that suck fat

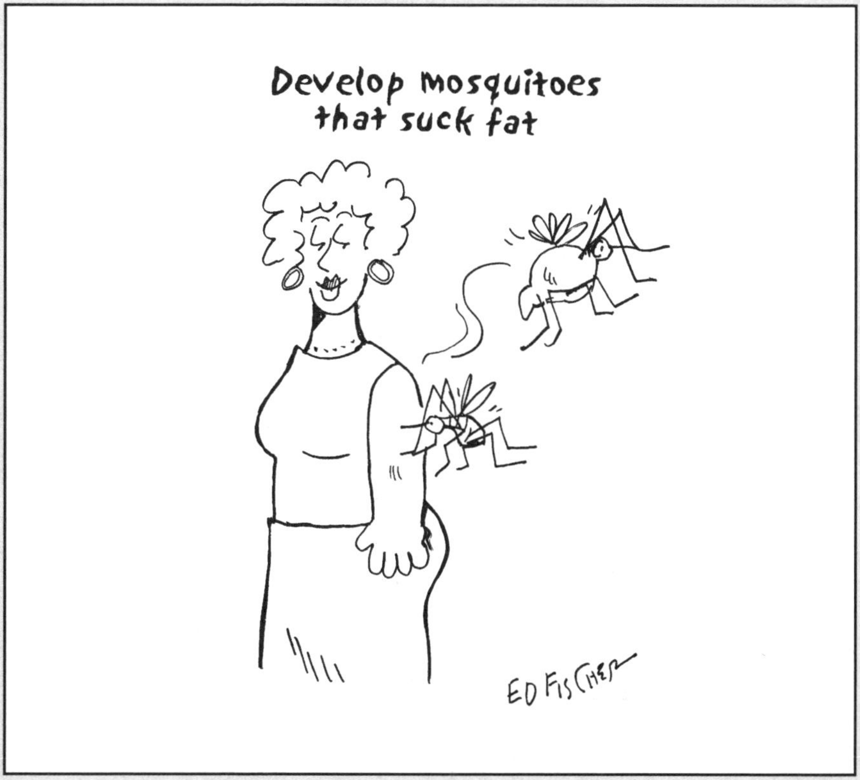
ED FISCHER

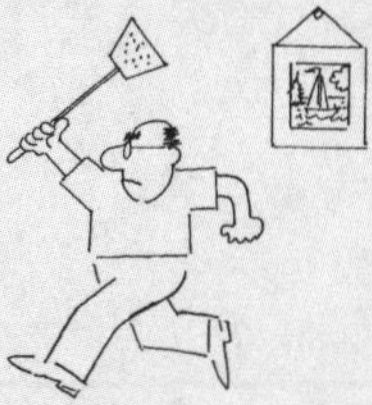

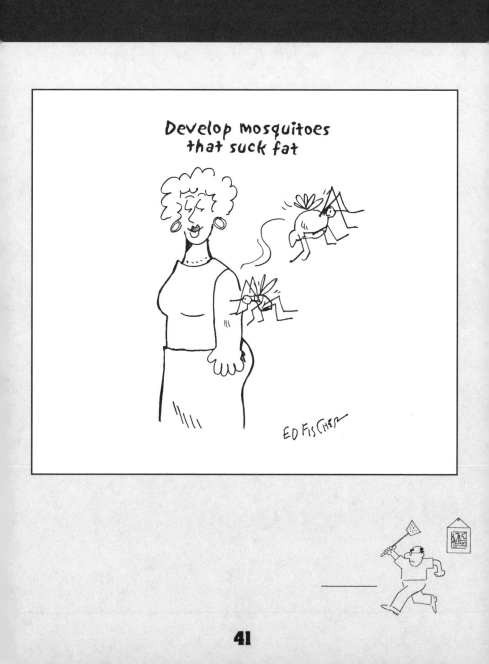

As long as they are going to buzz around the room, give them little feather dusters

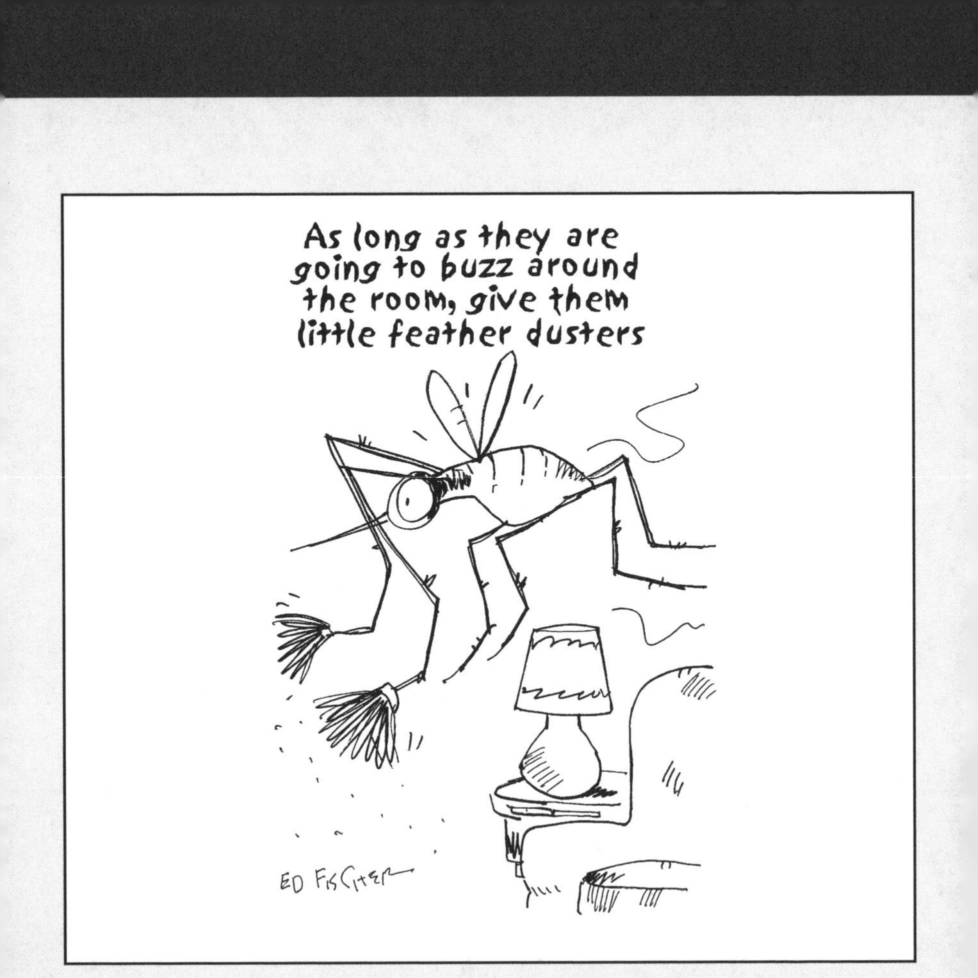
ED FISCHER

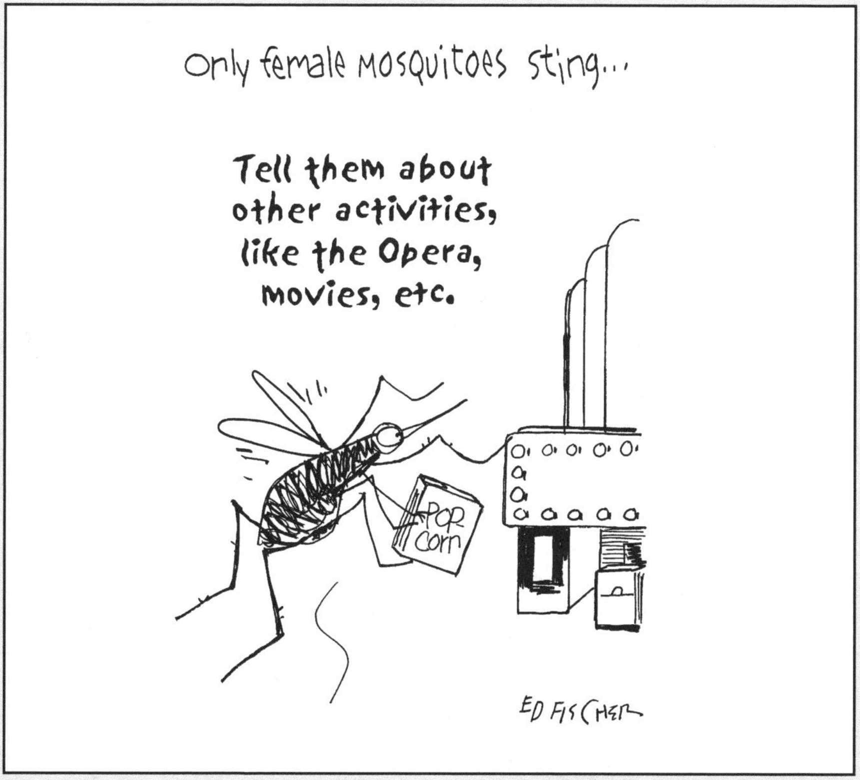
Only female mosquitoes sting...
Tell them about other activities, like the Opera, movies, etc.
POP corn
ED FISCHER

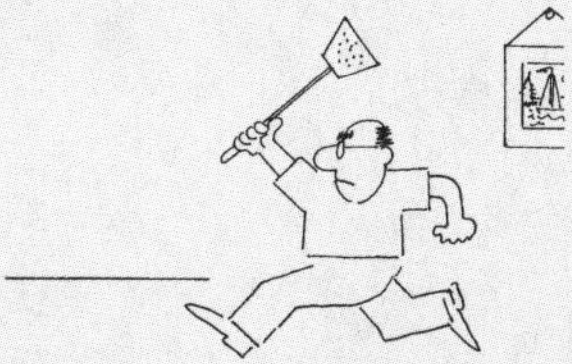

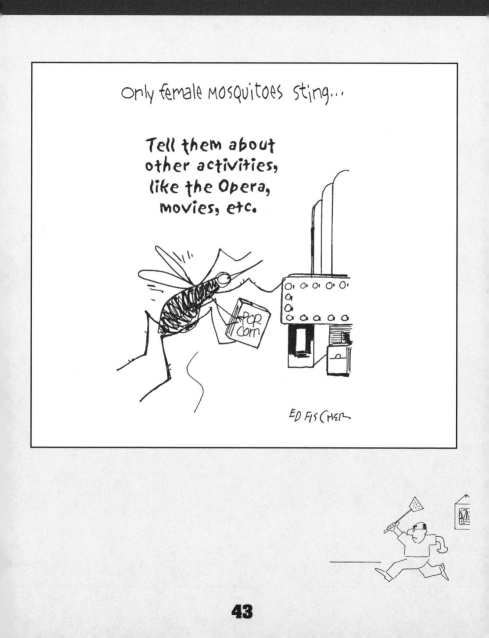

Train to fetch the paper

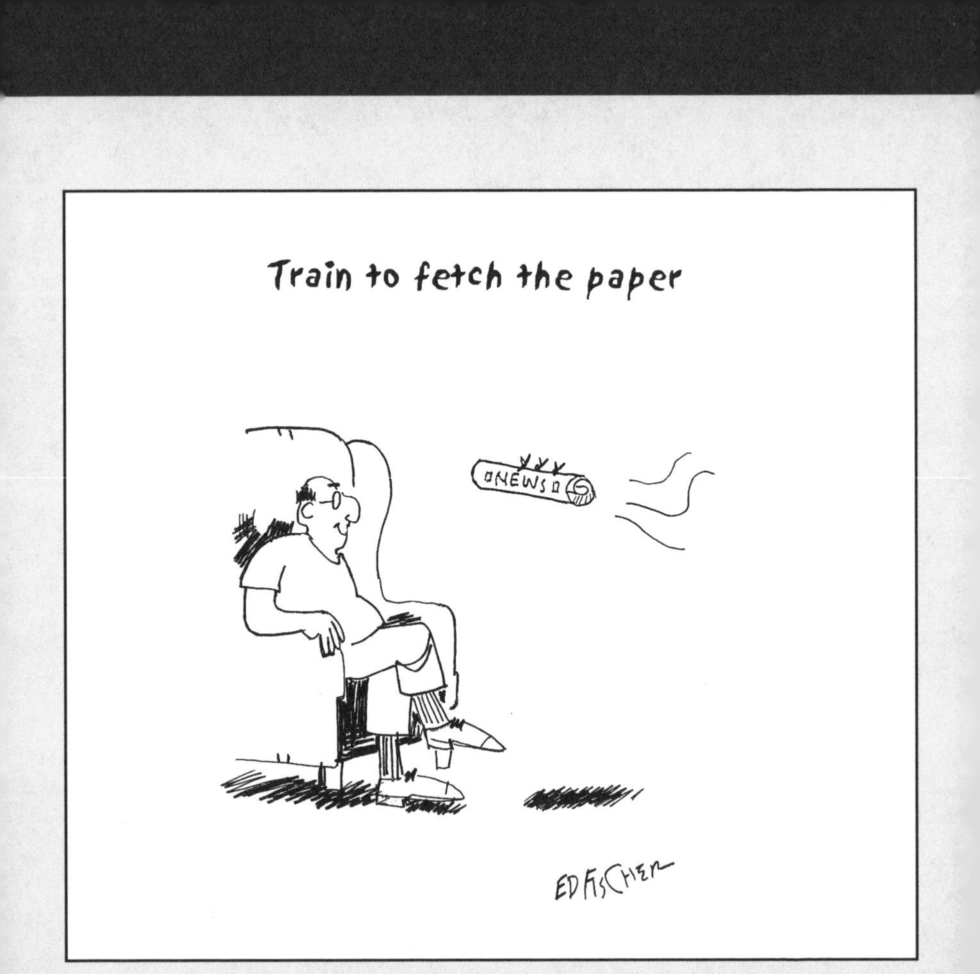
NEWS
ED FISCHER

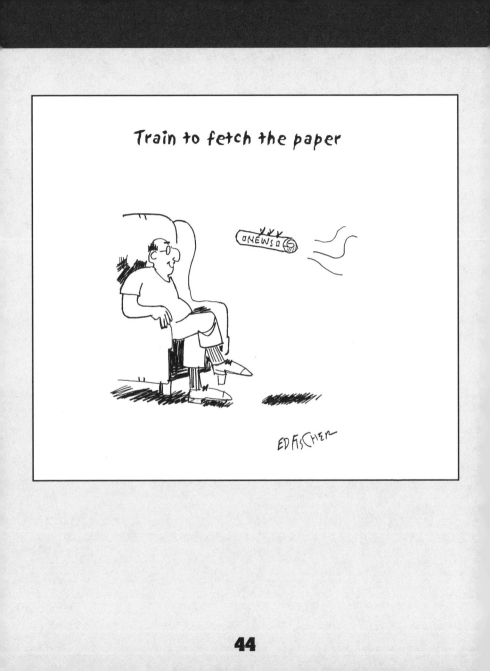

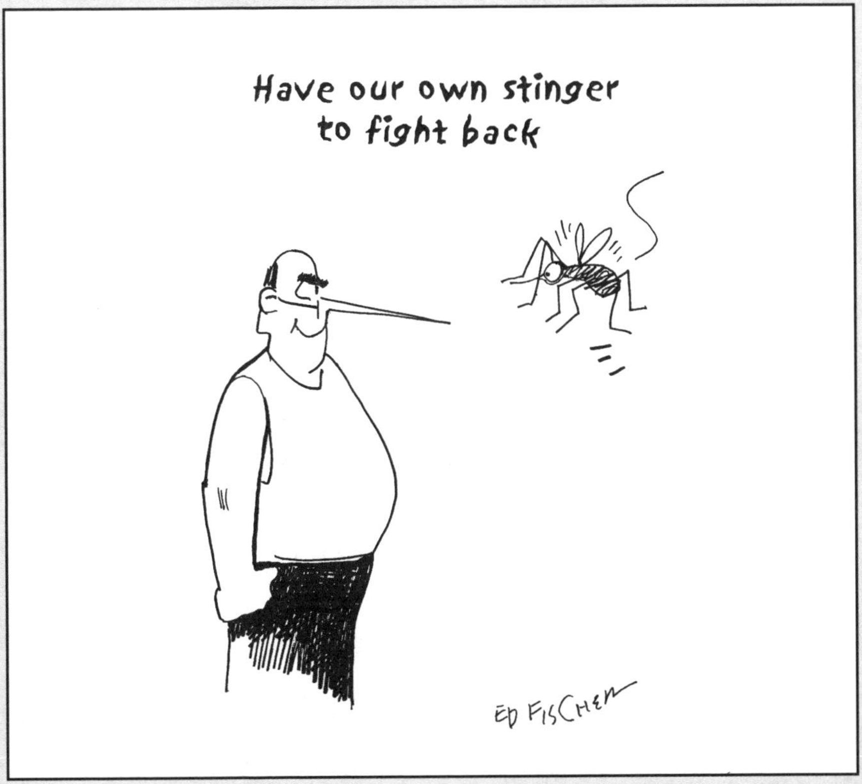
ED FISCHER

Have our own stinger
to fight back

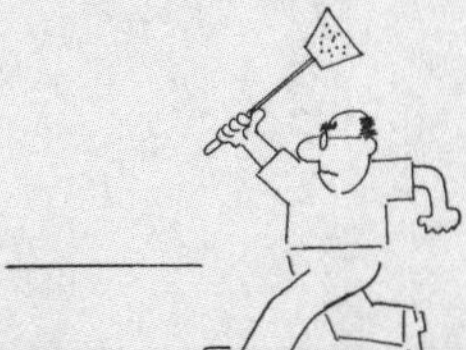

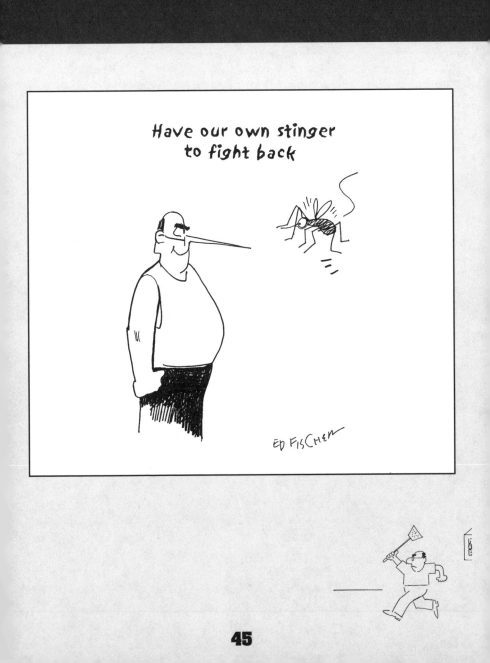

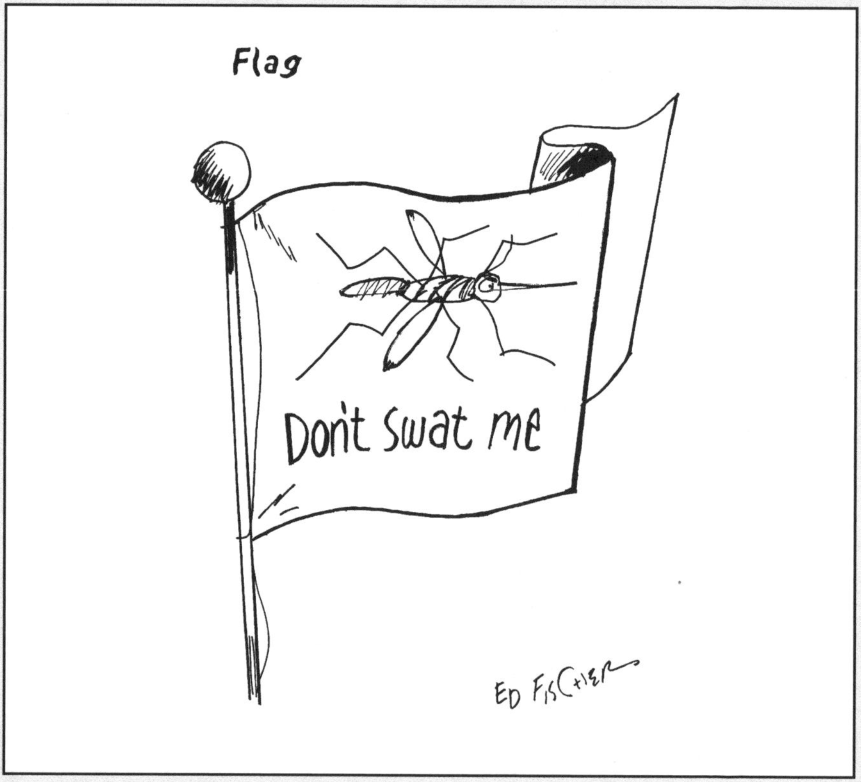
Flag
Don't swat me
ED FISCHER

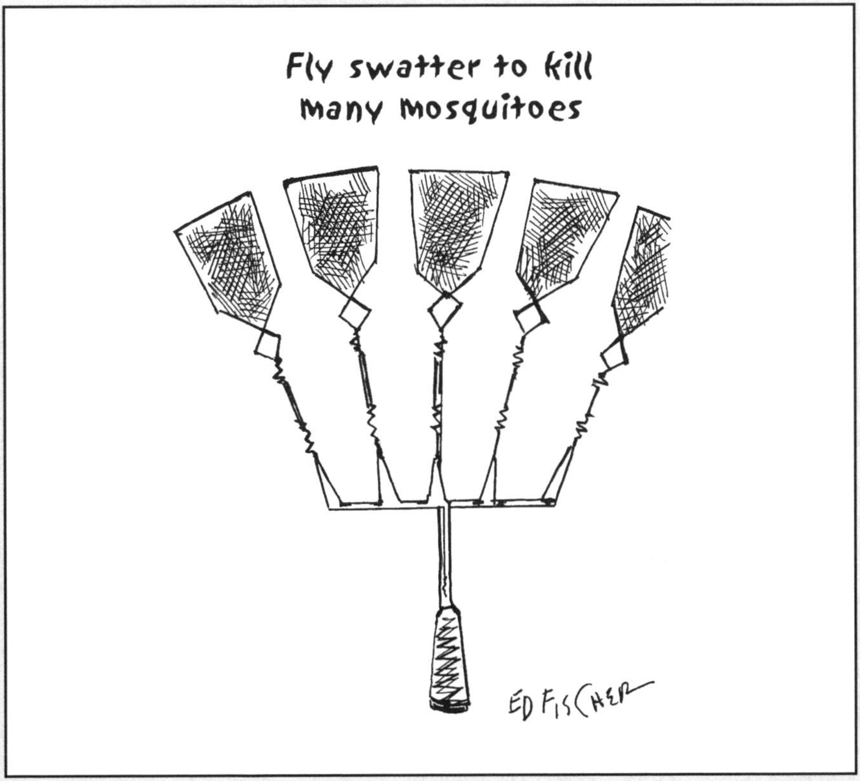
ED FISCHER

Fly swatter to kill
many mosquitoes

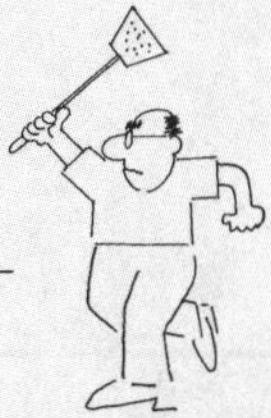

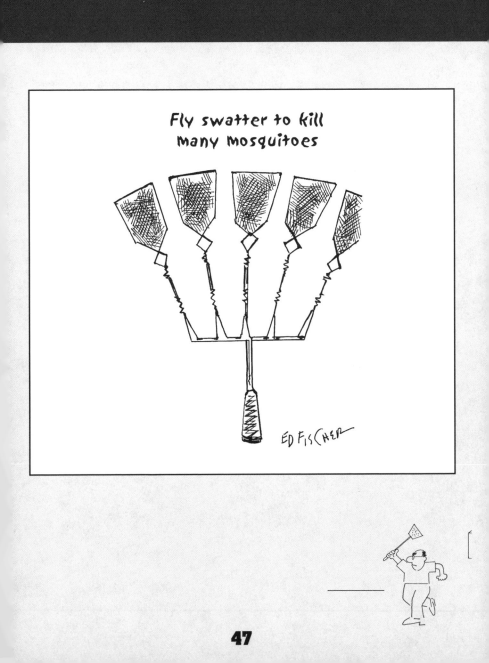

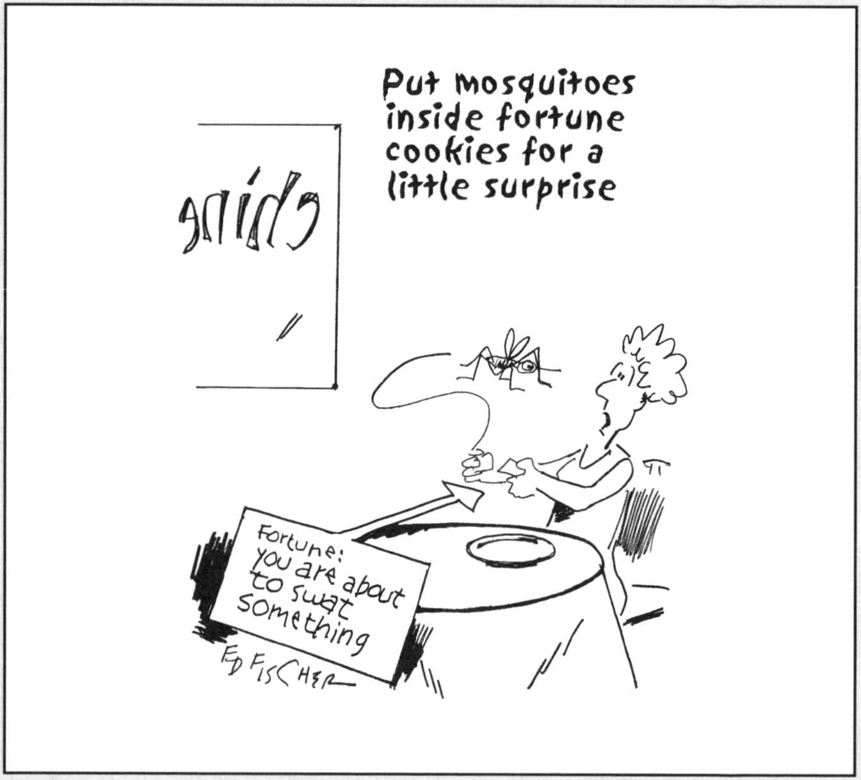
Put mosquitoes inside fortune cookies for a little surprise
Fortune: you are about to swat something
ED FISCHER

Show mosquitoes how to go south (and stay there)

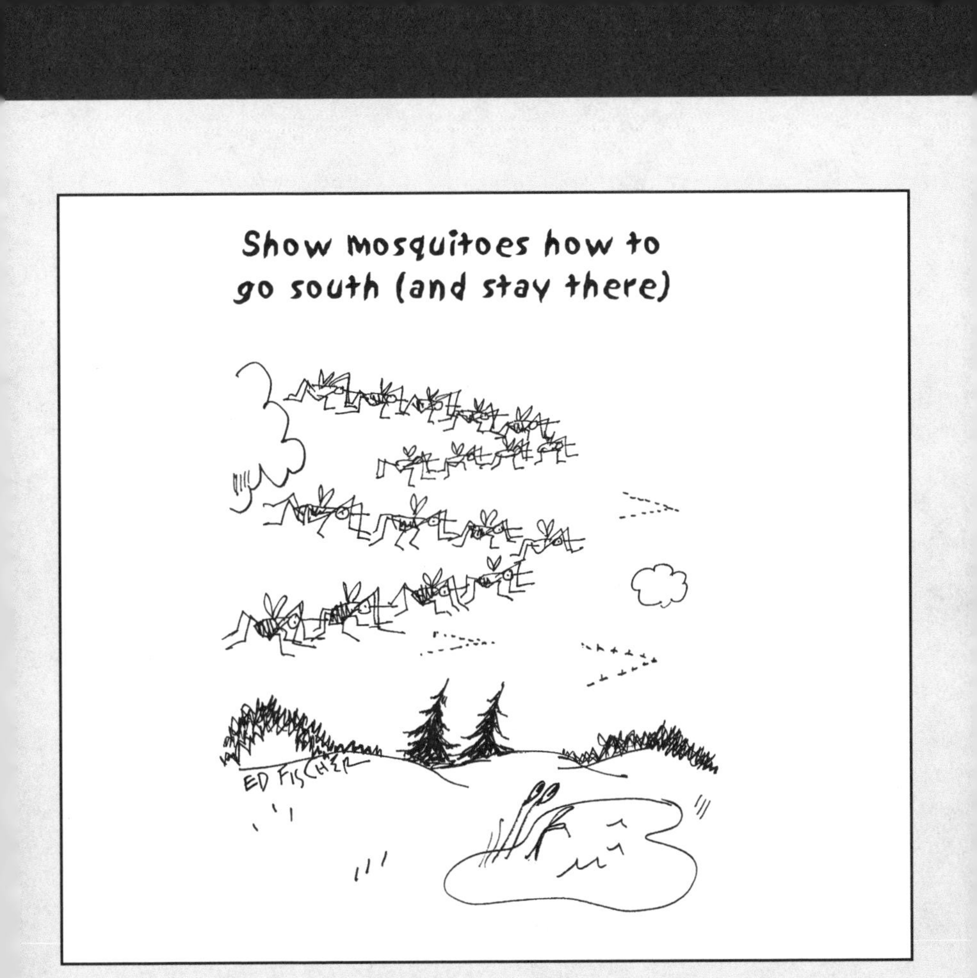
ED FISCHER

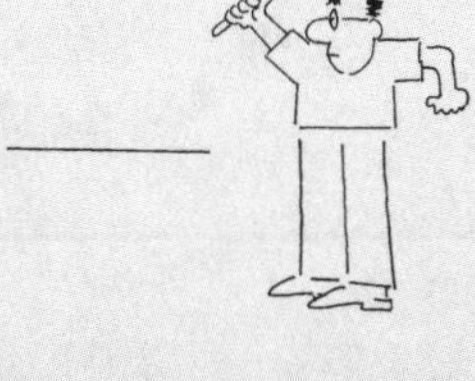

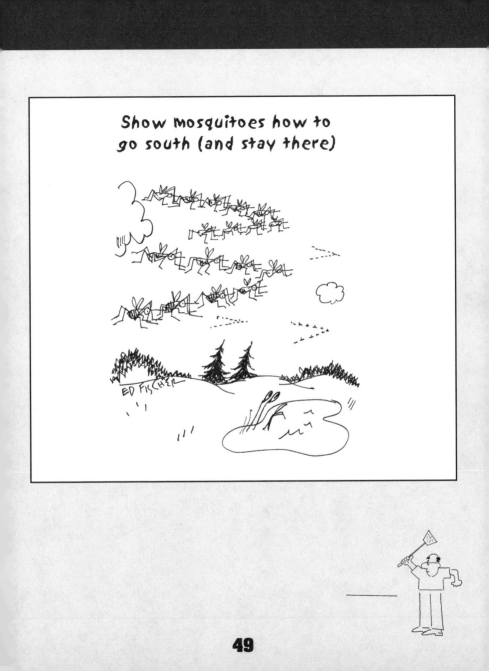

Unique hair brush

ED FISCHER

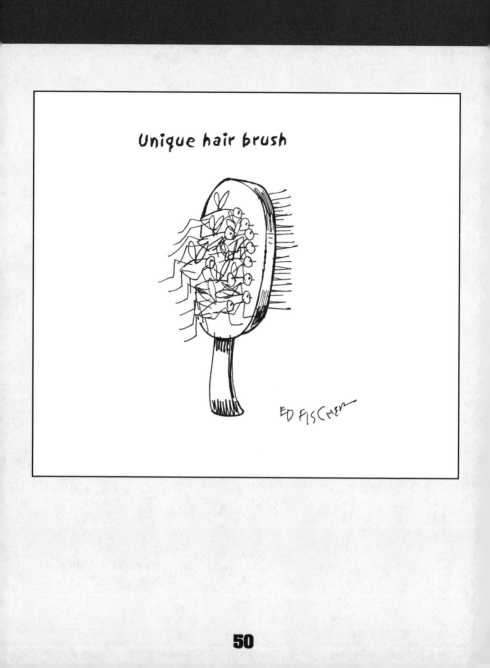

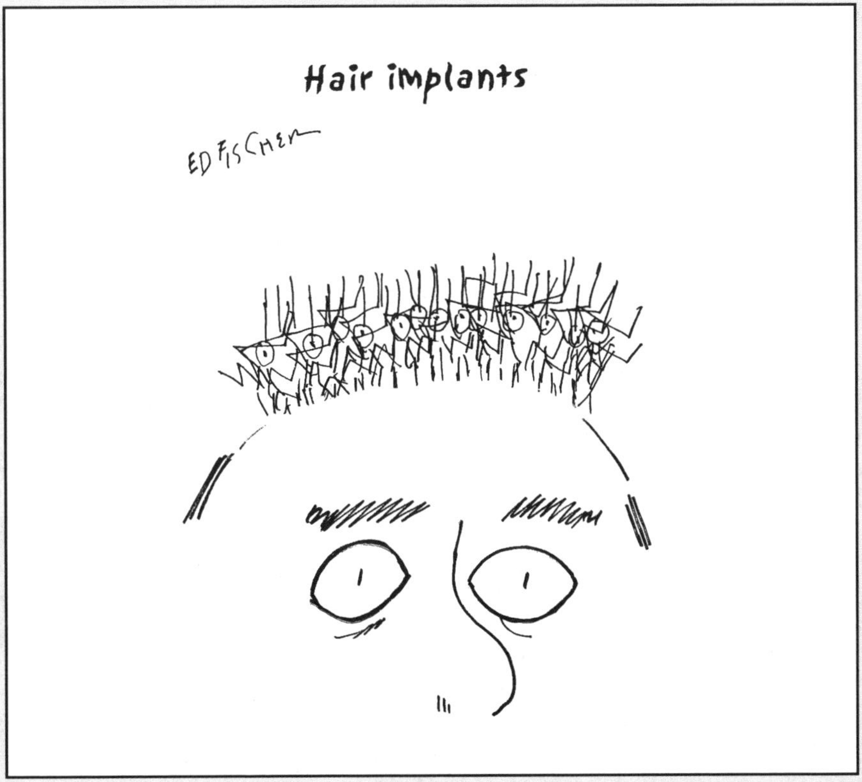
ED FISCHER

Hair implants

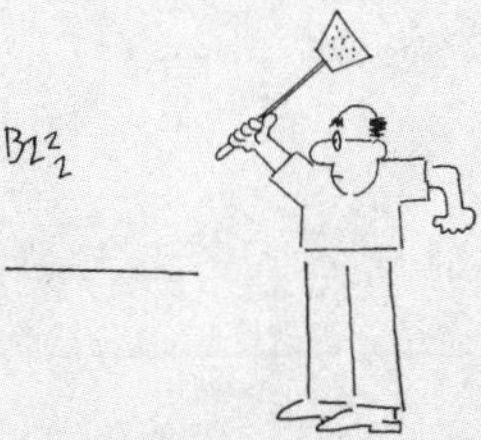
BZZZ

If they must buzz,
get them to harmonize

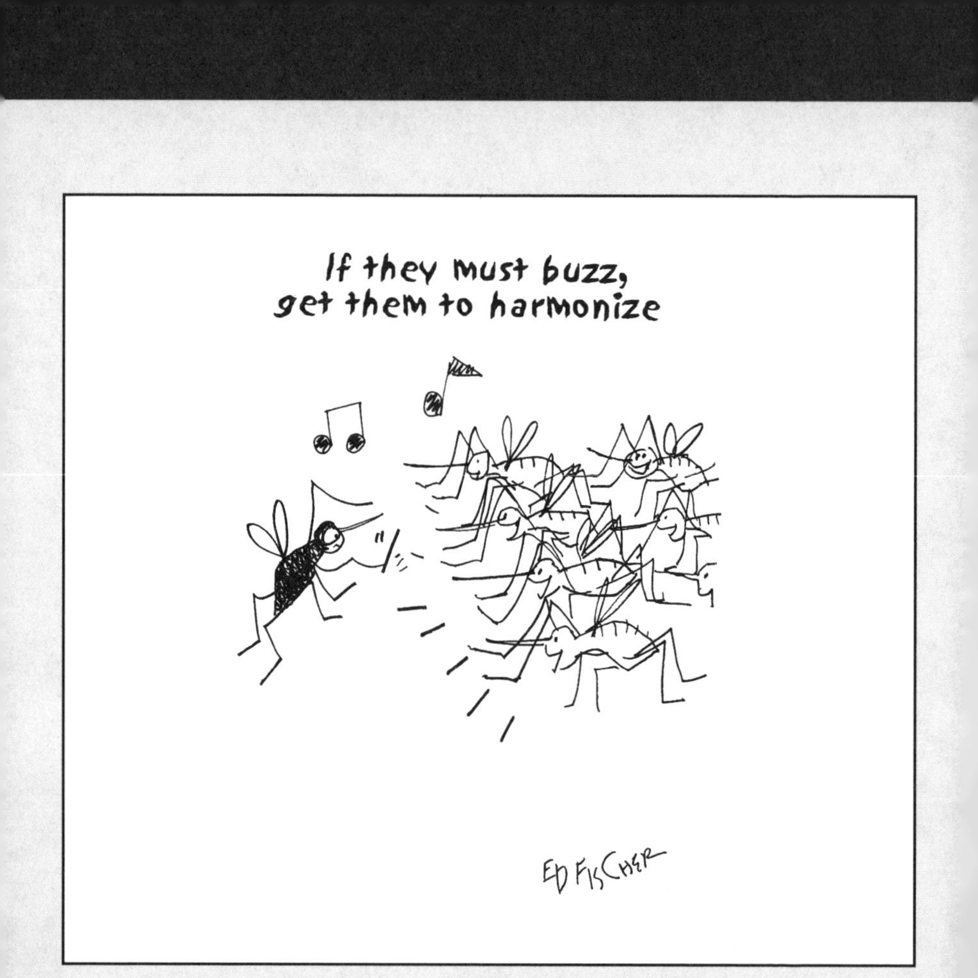
ED FISCHER

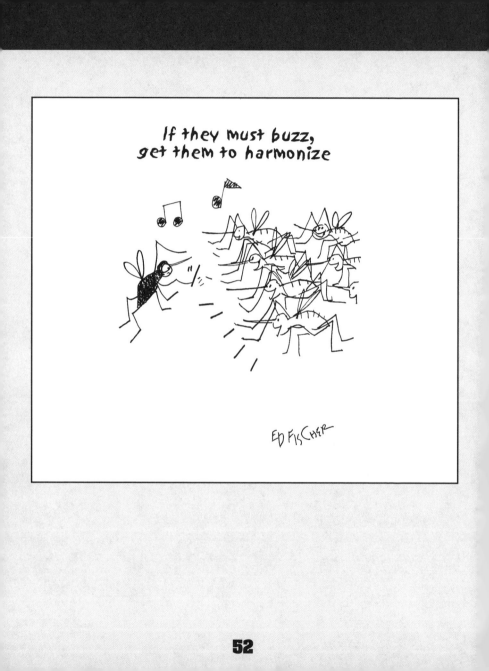

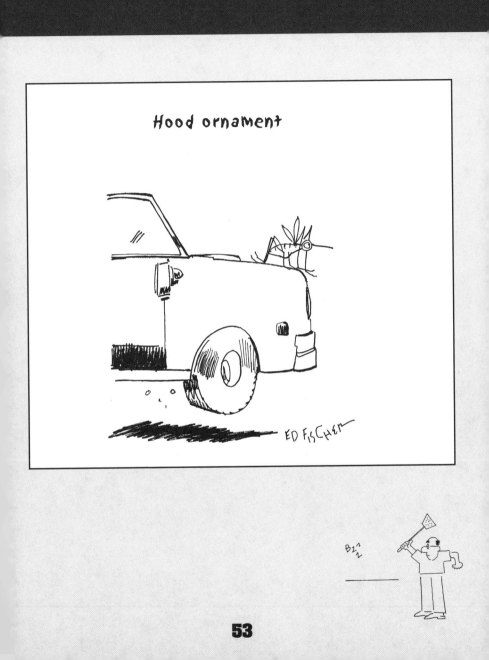

Hood ornament

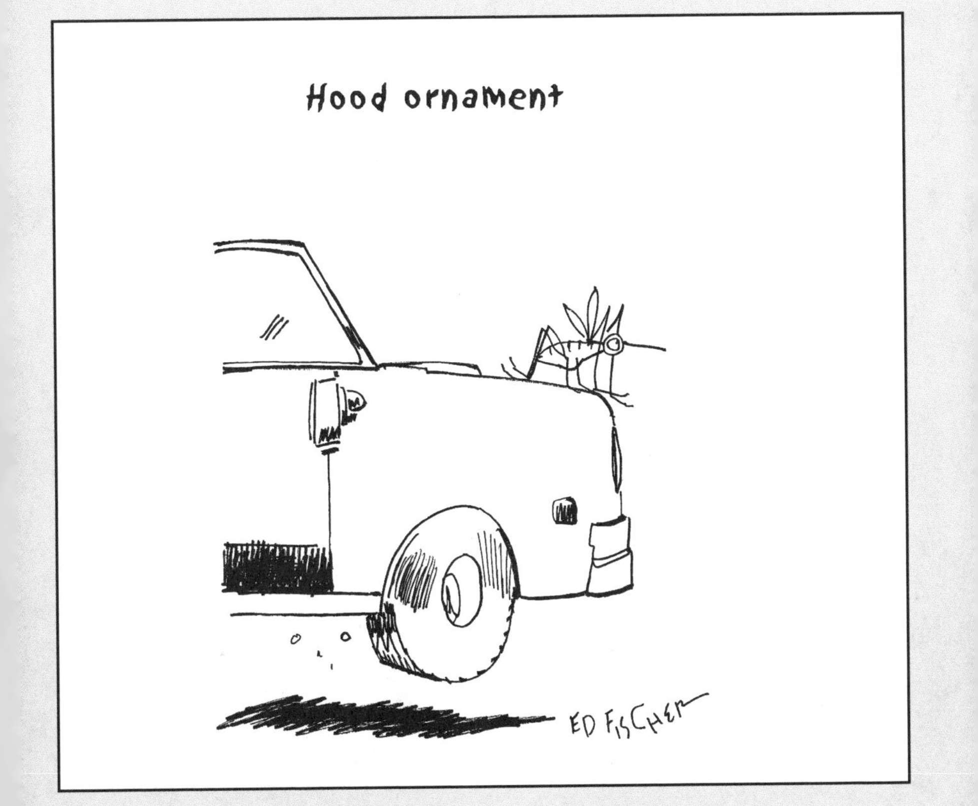
ED FISCHER

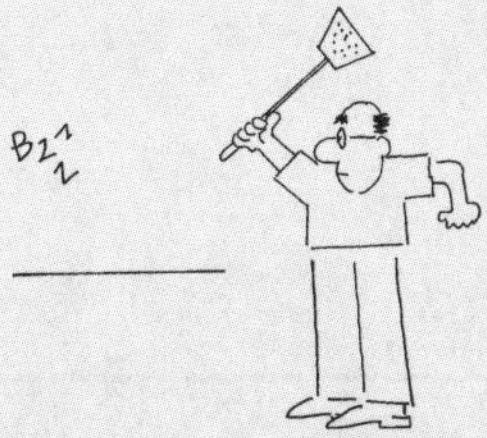

Hunt mosquitoes with decoys

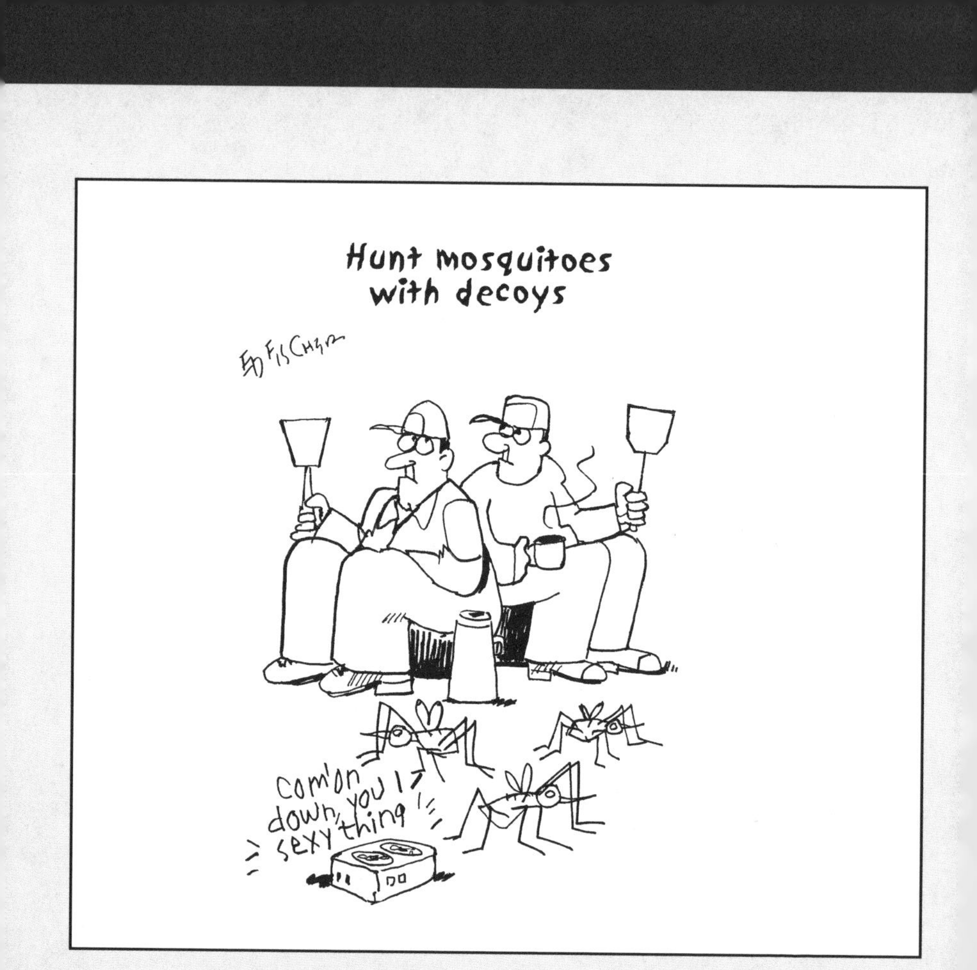
com'on down, you sexy thing

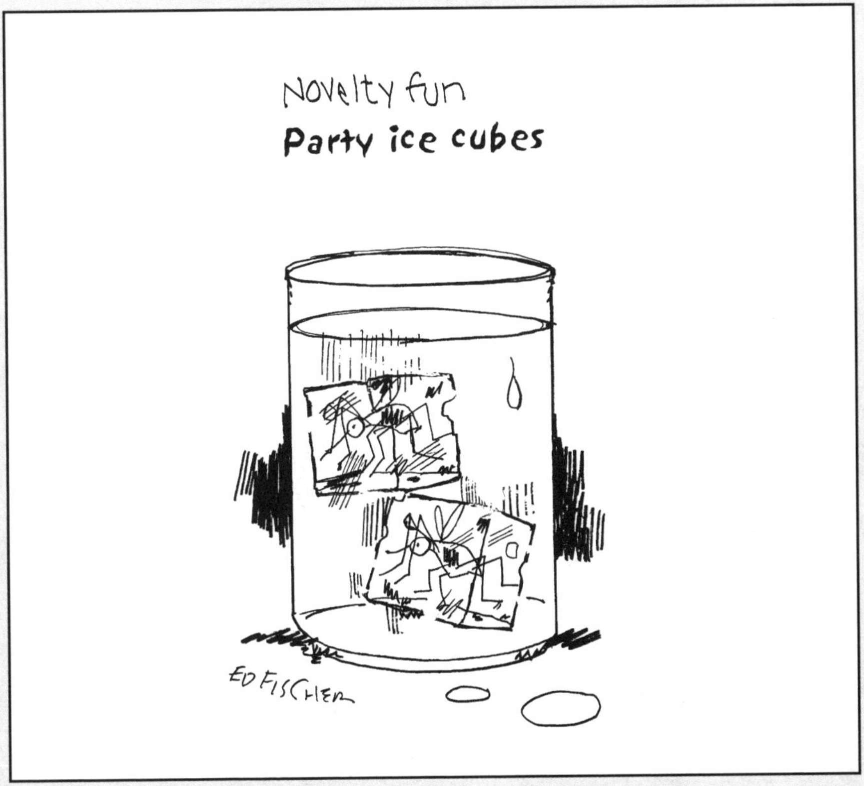
Novelty fun
Party ice cubes
ED FISCHER

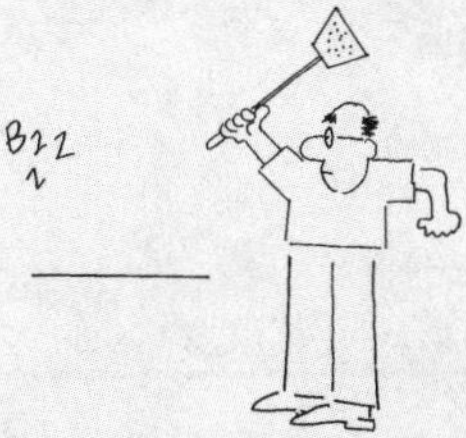

Share our mosquitoes...

Send them along with
your taxes to the I.R.S.

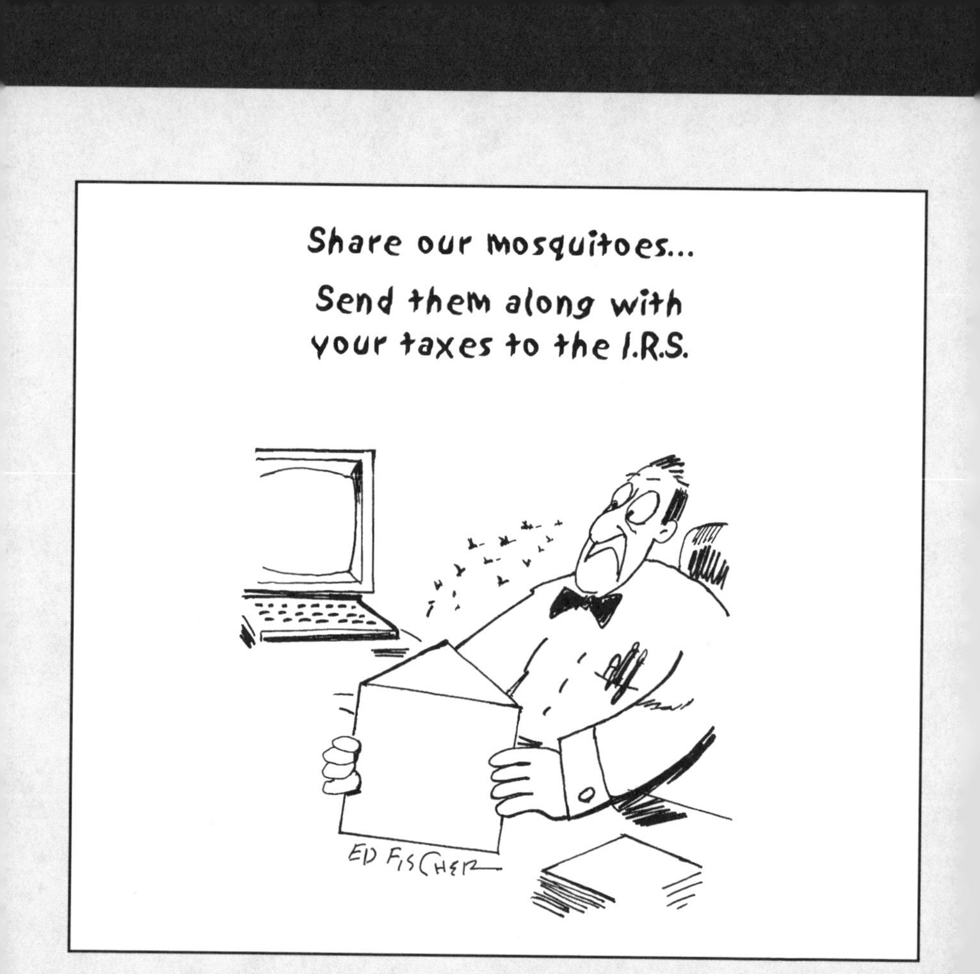
ED FISCHER

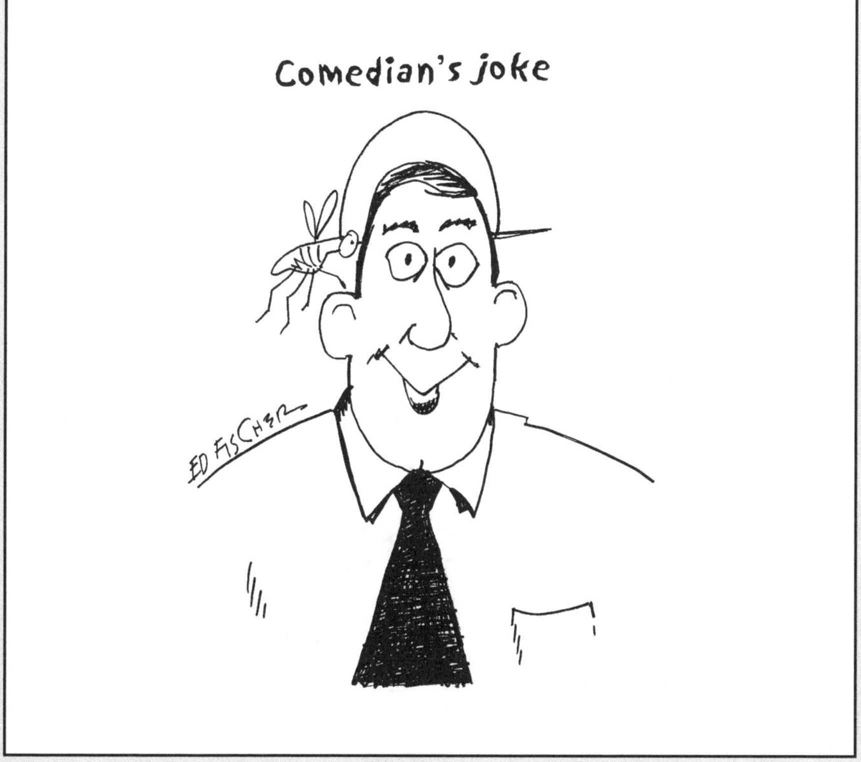
Comedian's joke
ED FISCHER

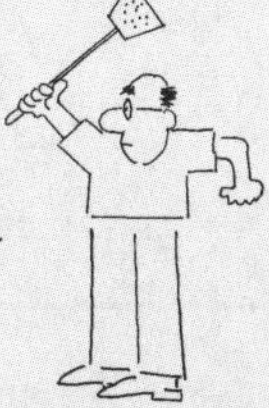

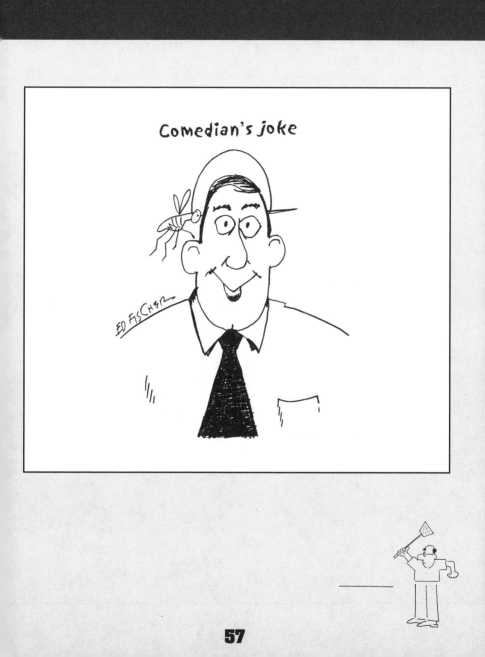

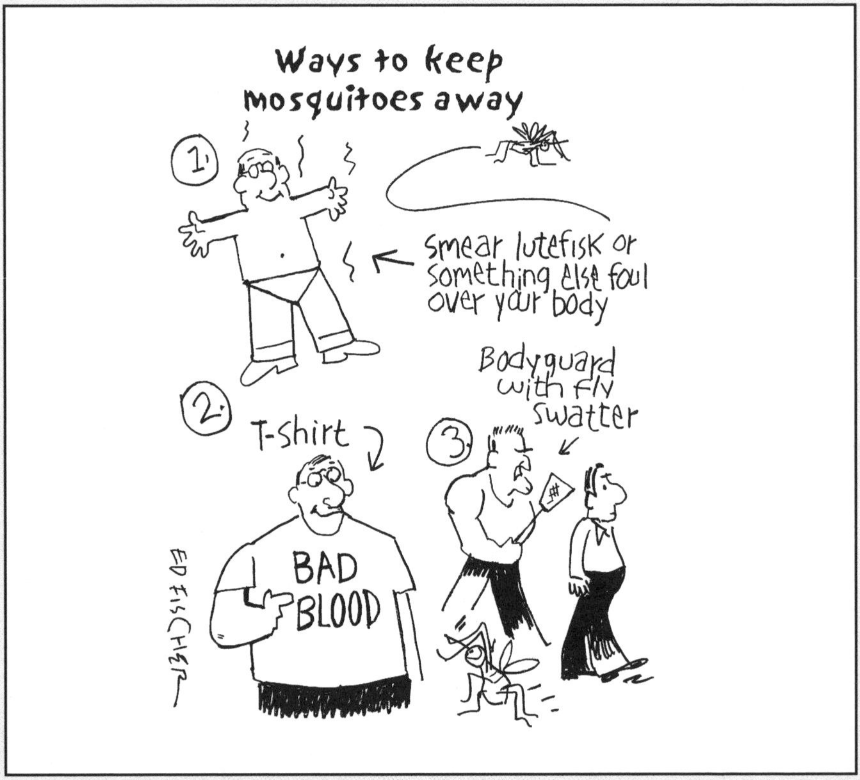
Ways to keep mosquitoes away
1.
Smear lutefisk or something else foul over your body
2.
T-shirt
BAD BLOOD
3.
Bodyguard with fly swatter
ED FISCHER

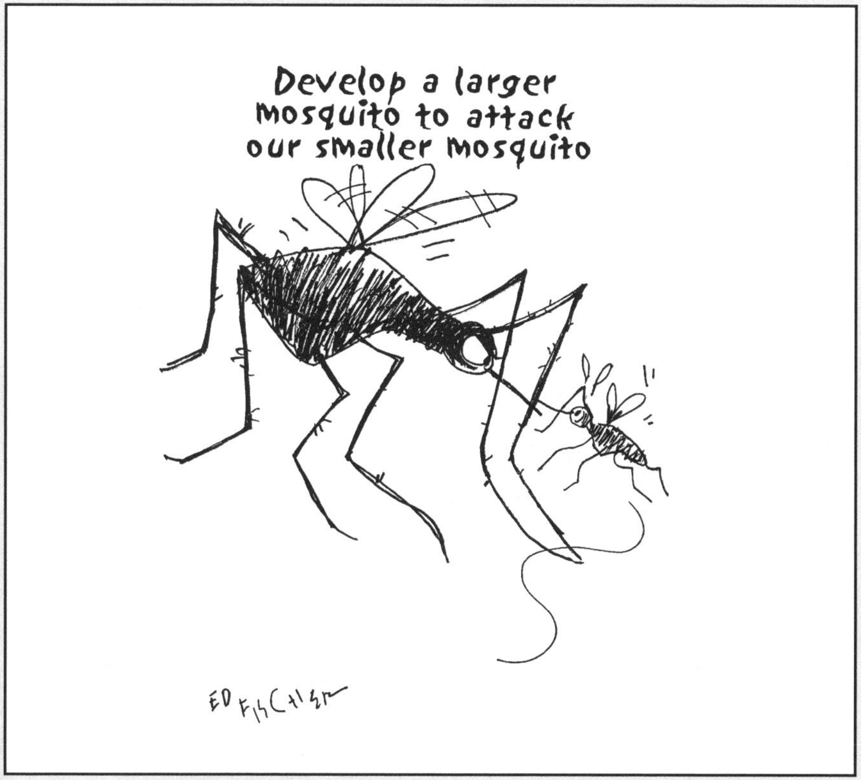
Develop a larger mosquito to attack our smaller mosquito
ED FISCHER

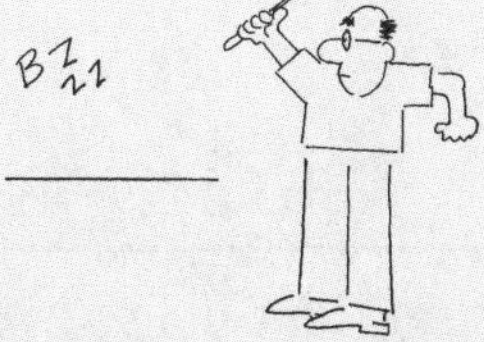
BZZZ

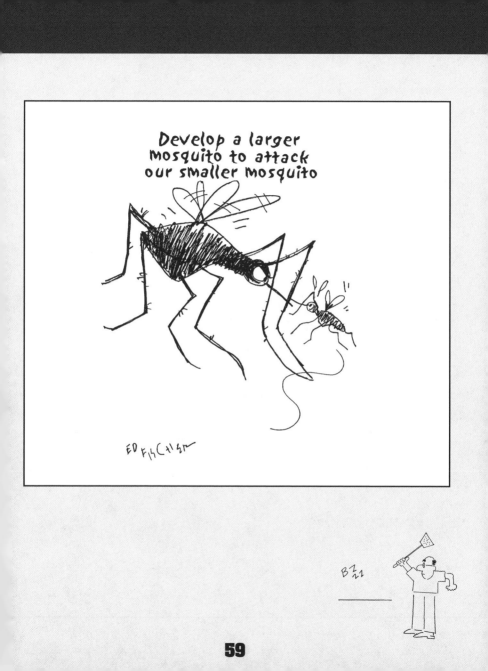

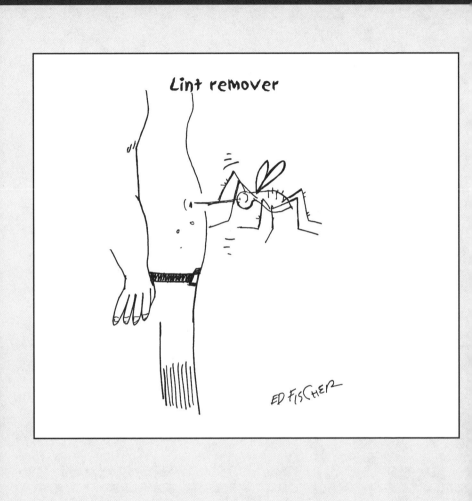

Lint remover

ED FISCHER

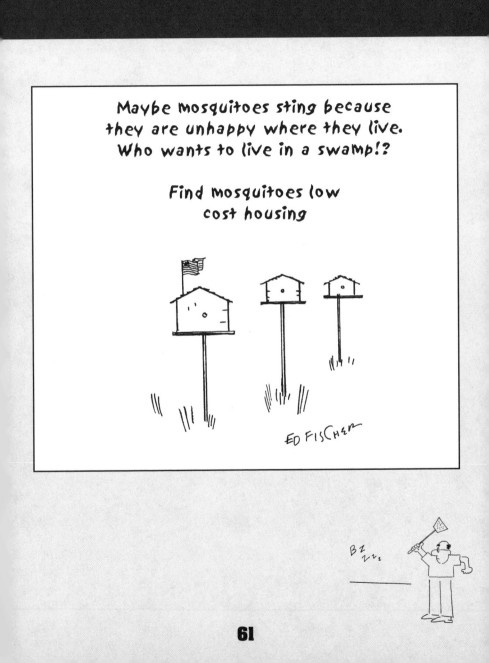

Maybe mosquitoes sting because they are unhappy where they live. Who wants to live in a swamp!?

Find mosquitoes low cost housing

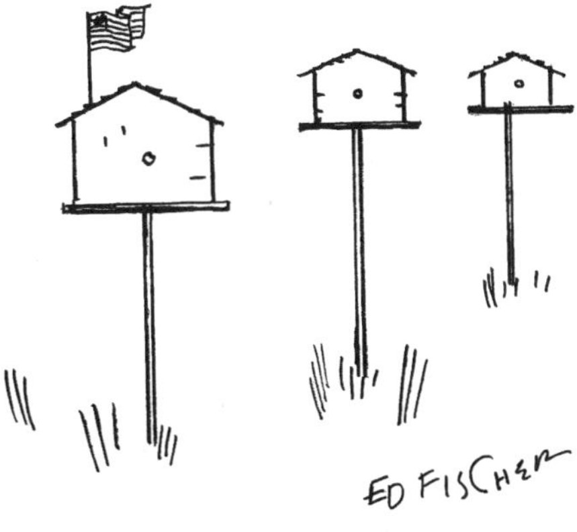
ED FISCHER

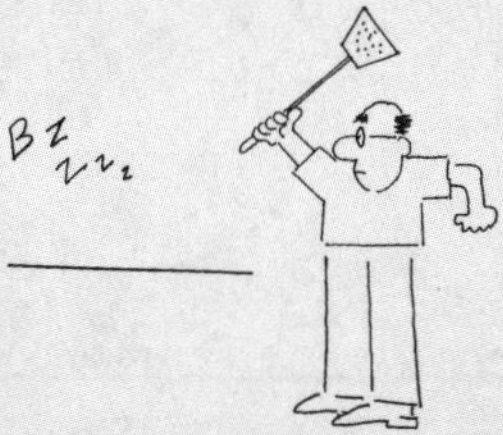
BZ zzz

To make a bull extra mad

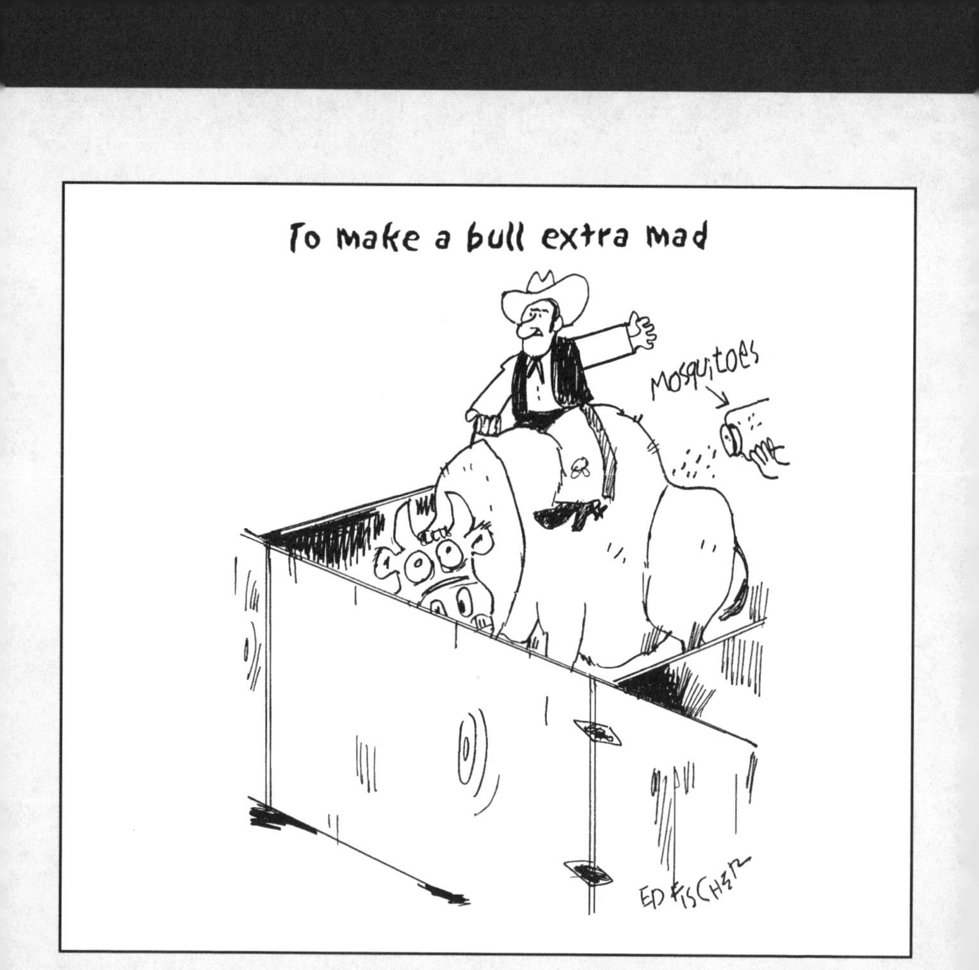
Mosquitoes
ED FISCHER

Only female mosquitoes sting

Have a way to identify male mosquitoes

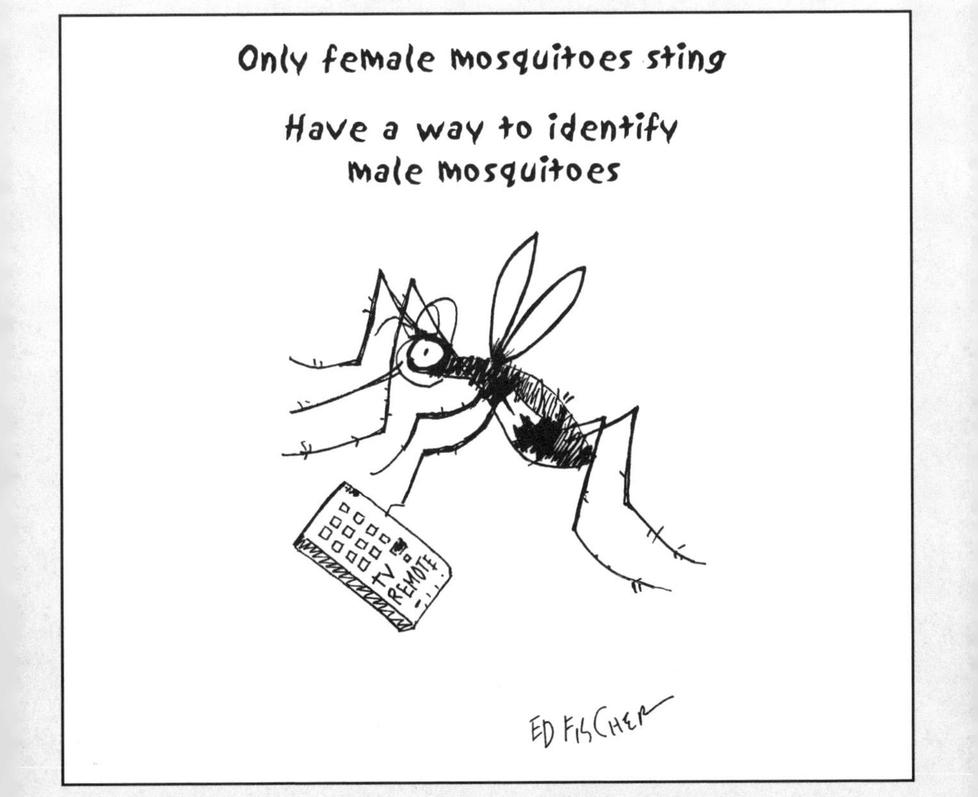
TV REMOTE
ED FISCHER

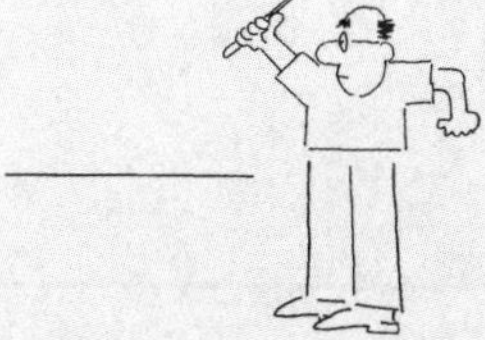

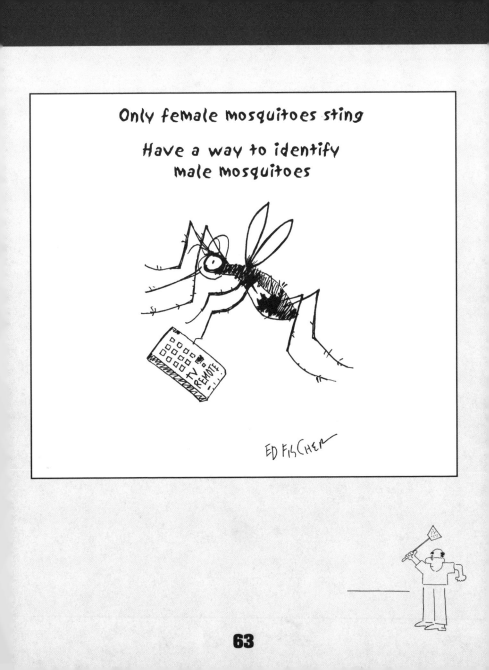

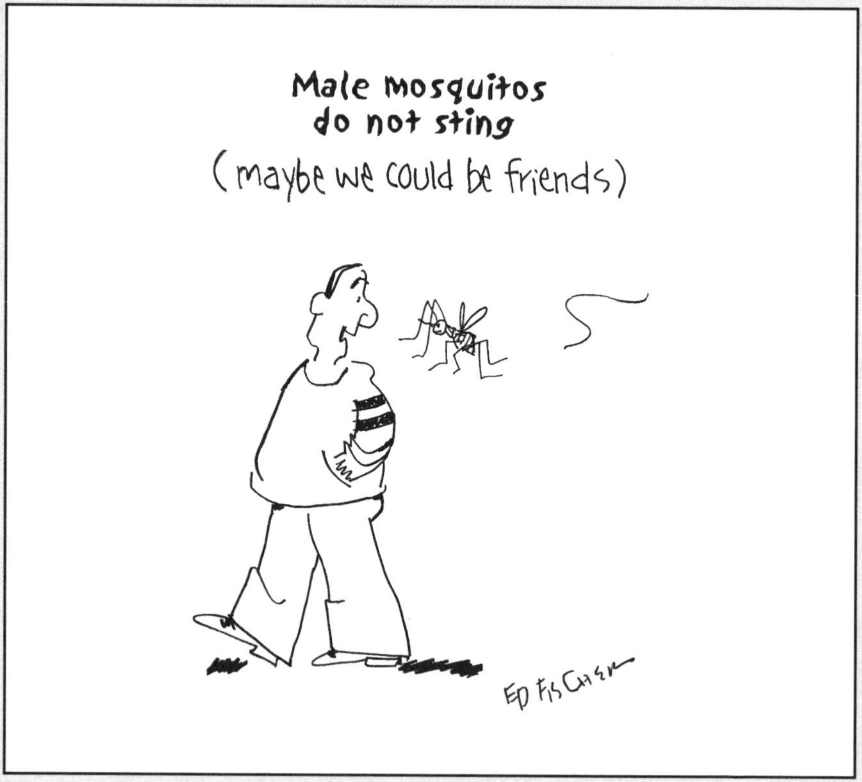
Male mosquitos
do not sting
(maybe we could be friends)
ED FISCHER

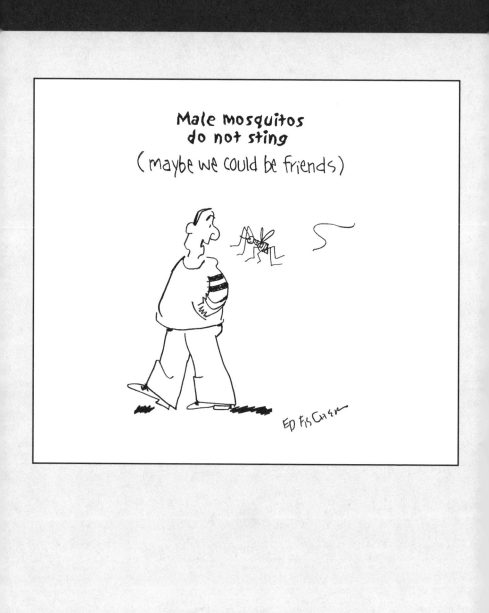

Marketing possibilities

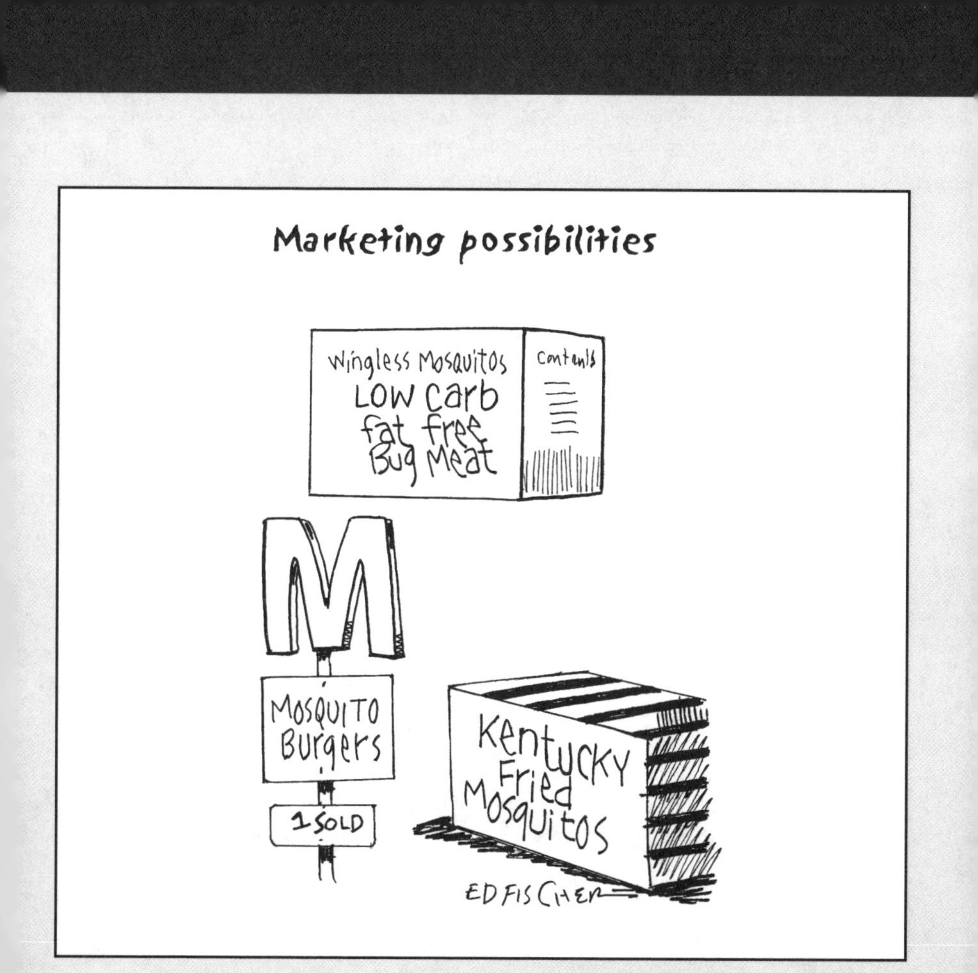
Wingless Mosquitos
LOW Carb
fat free
Bug Meat
Contents
M
MOSQUITO
Burgers
1 SOLD
Kentucky
Fried
Mosquitos
ED FISCHER

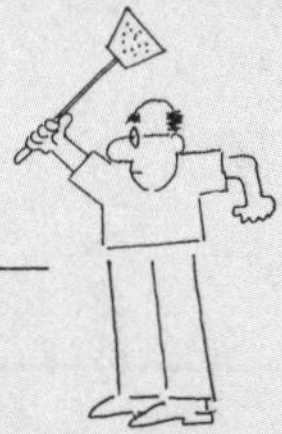

Just a thought...

Why isn't there a mosquito mascot?

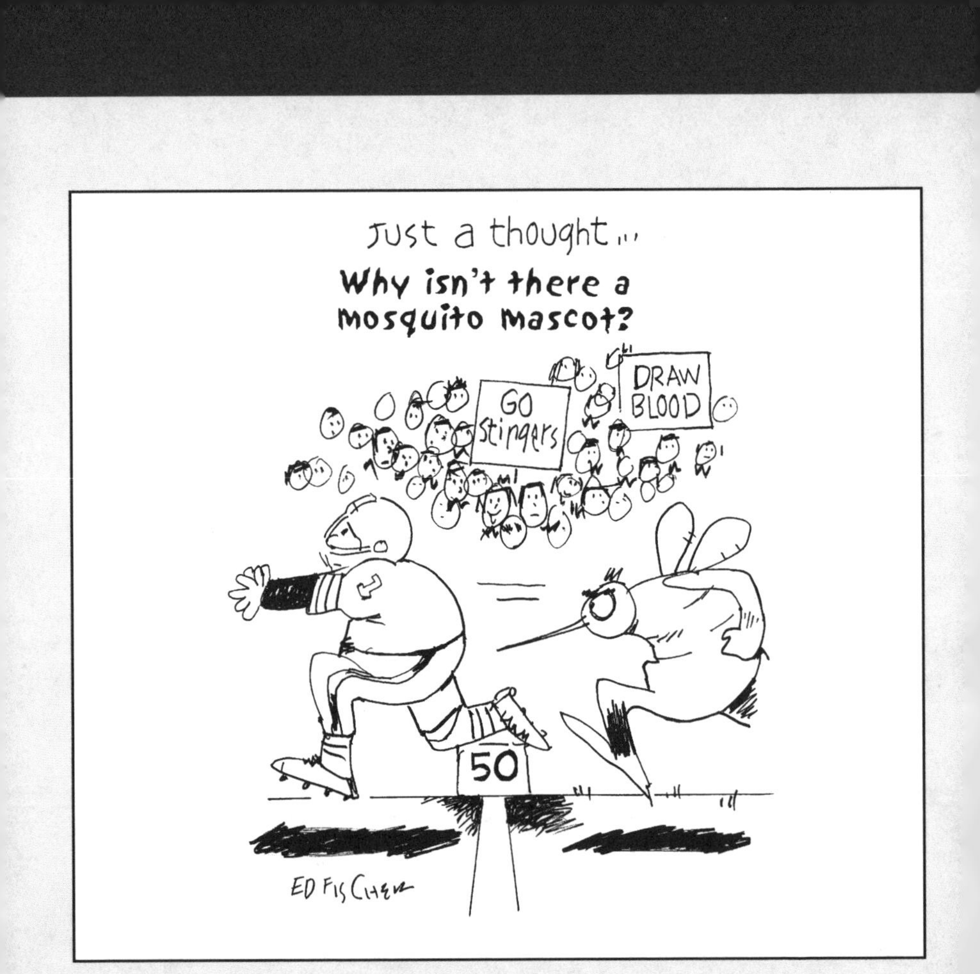
GO Stingers
DRAW BLOOD
50
ED FISCHER

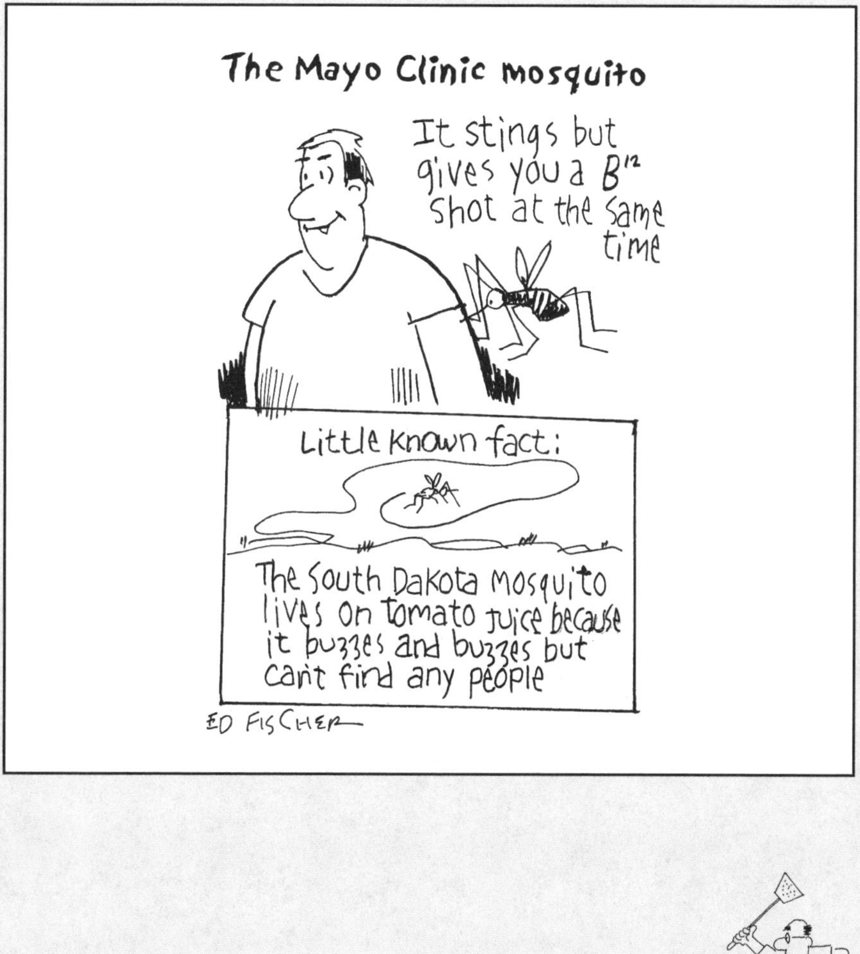
The Mayo Clinic mosquito
It stings but gives you a B12 shot at the same time
Little known fact:
The South Dakota mosquito lives on tomato juice because it buzzes and buzzes but can't find any people
ED FISCHER

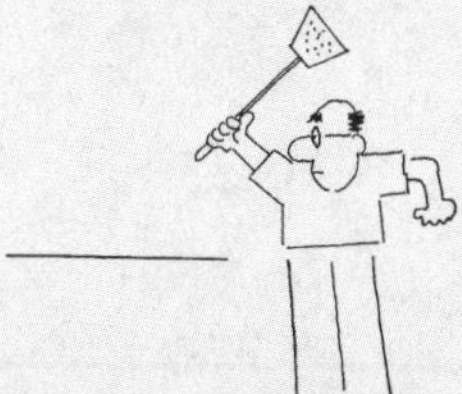

Give medals for big mosquito kills

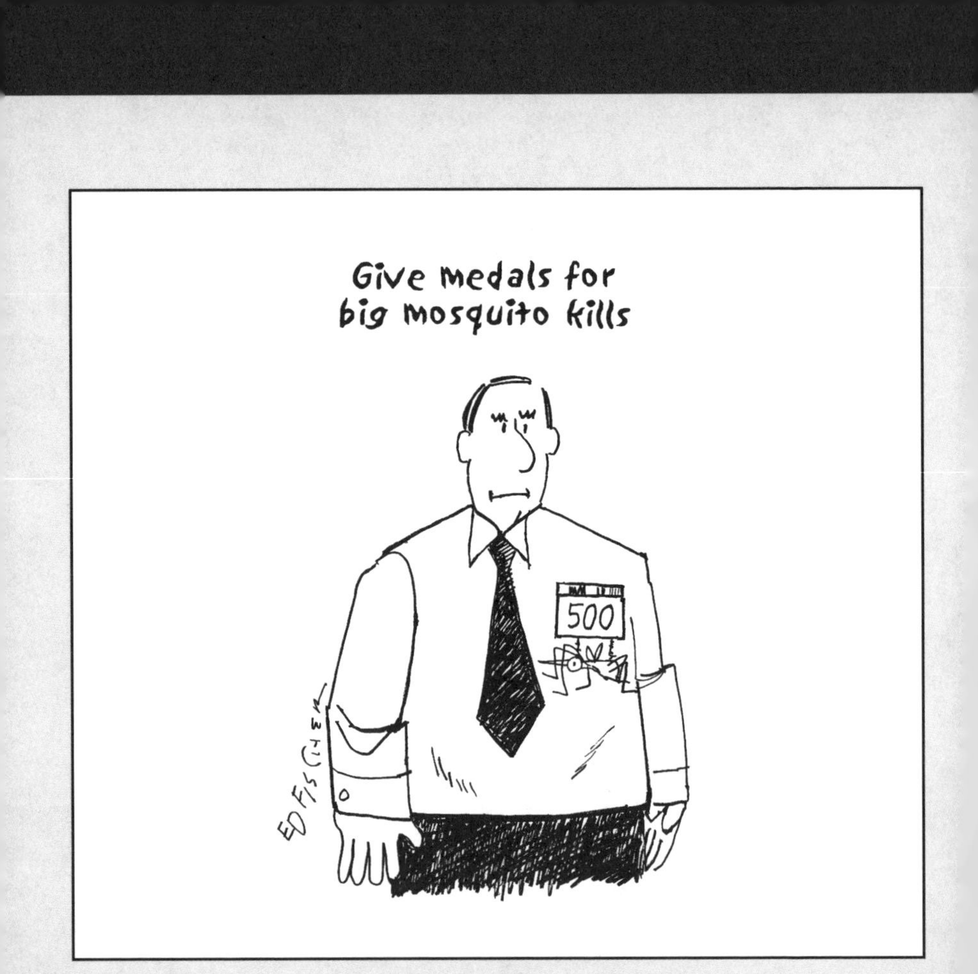
500
ED FISCHER

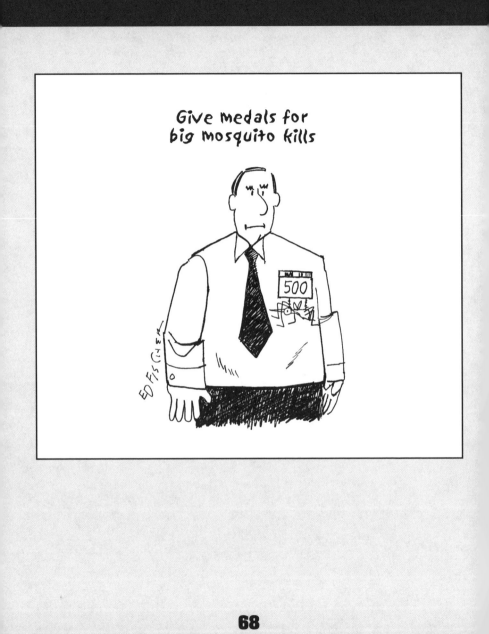

Mosquito tank instead of fish tank

give them names

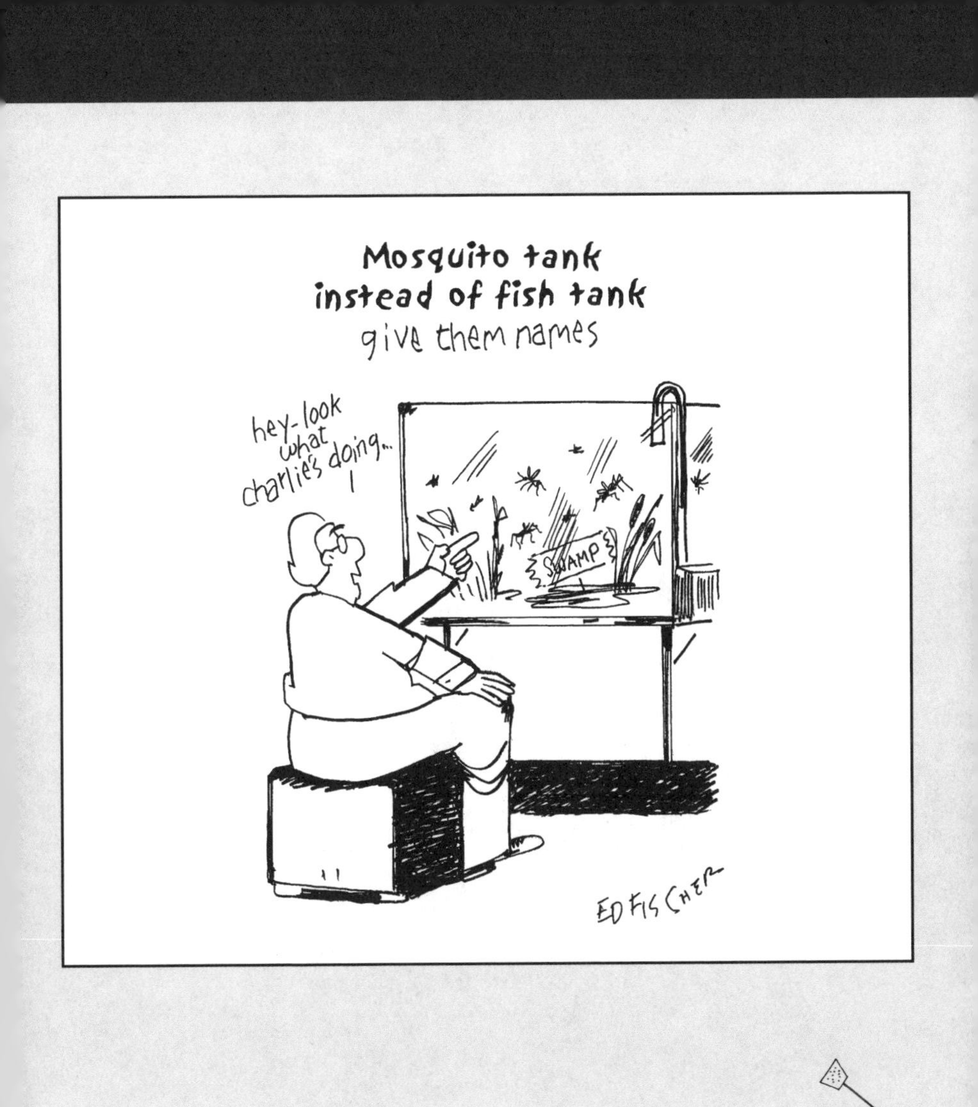
hey-look what charlie's doing...
SWAMP
ED FISCHER

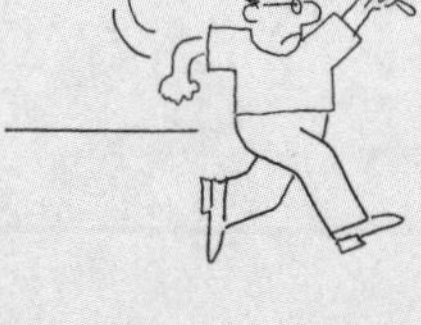

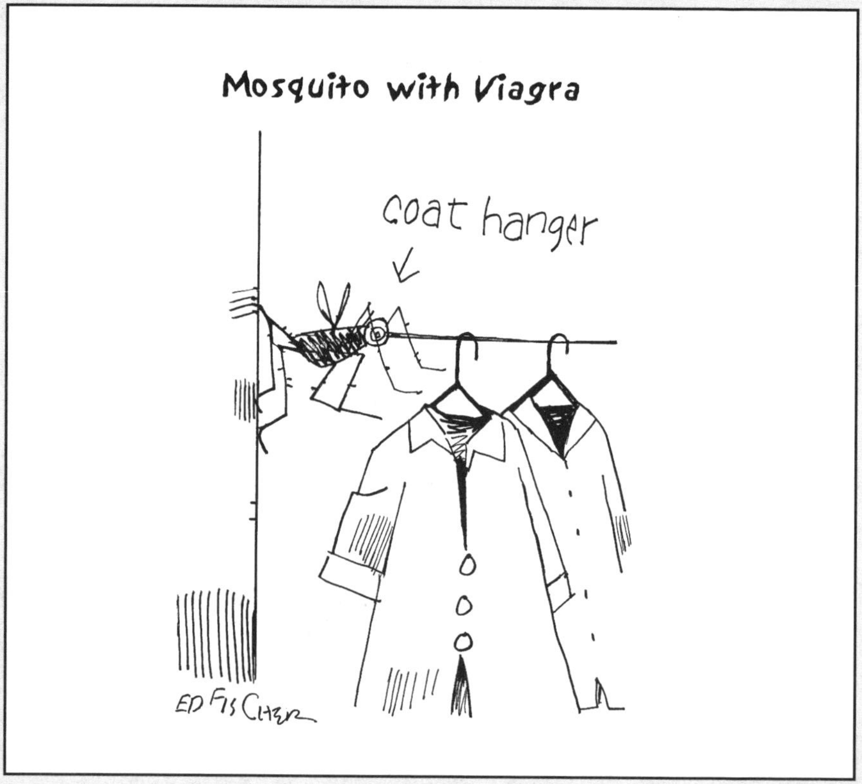
Mosquito with Viagra
coat hanger
ED FISCHER

Hands-free nose picker

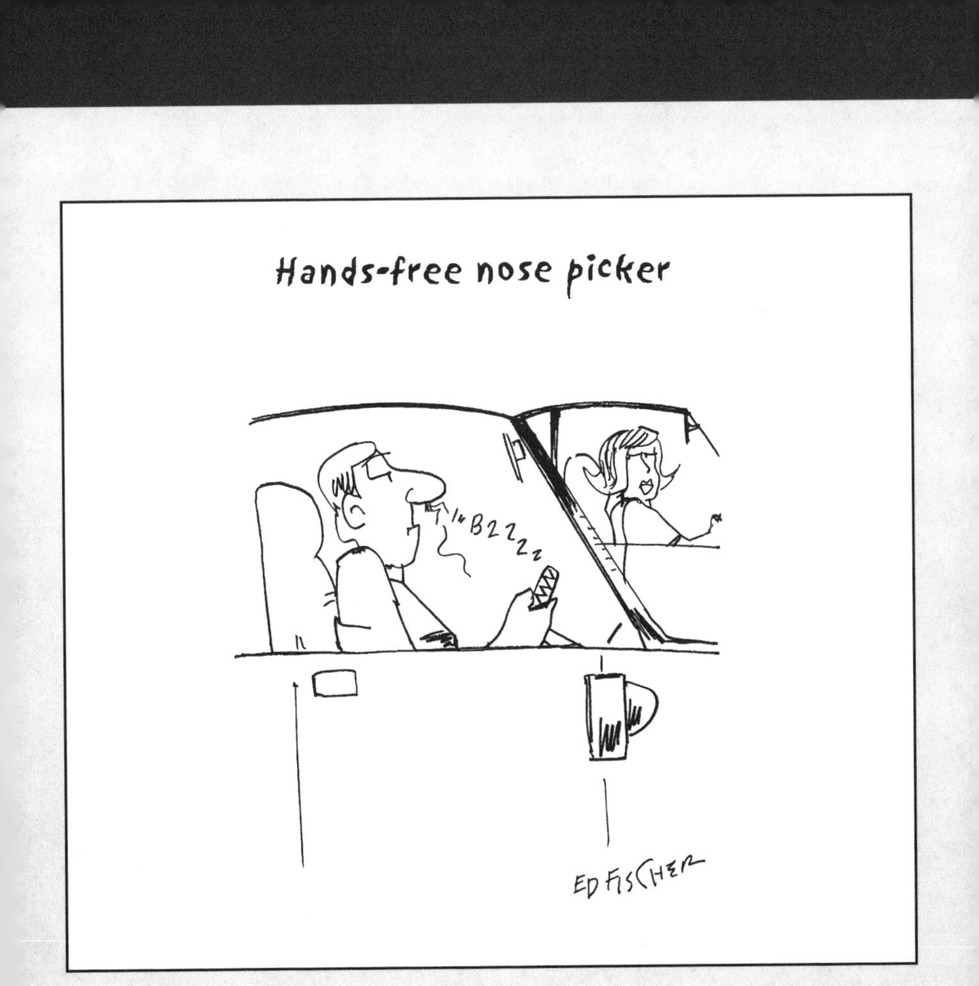
BZZZZ
ED FISCHER

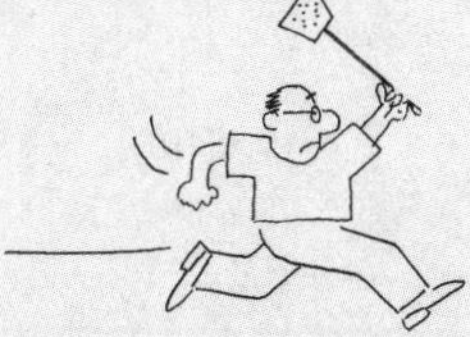

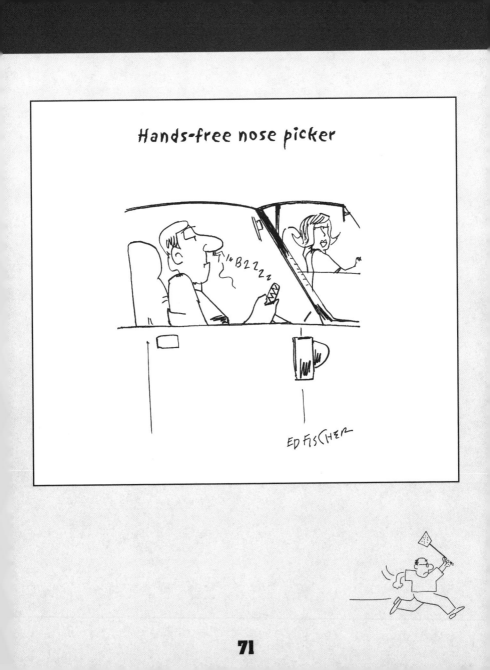

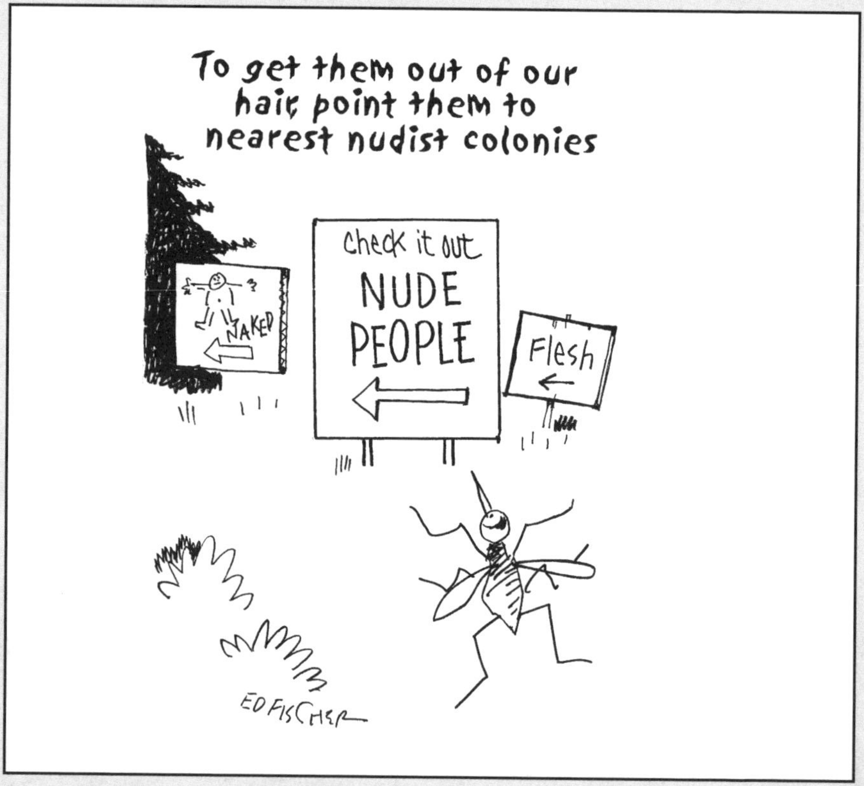
To get them out of our hair, point them to nearest nudist colonies
NAKED
check it out
NUDE PEOPLE
Flesh
ED FISCHER

For older mosquitos

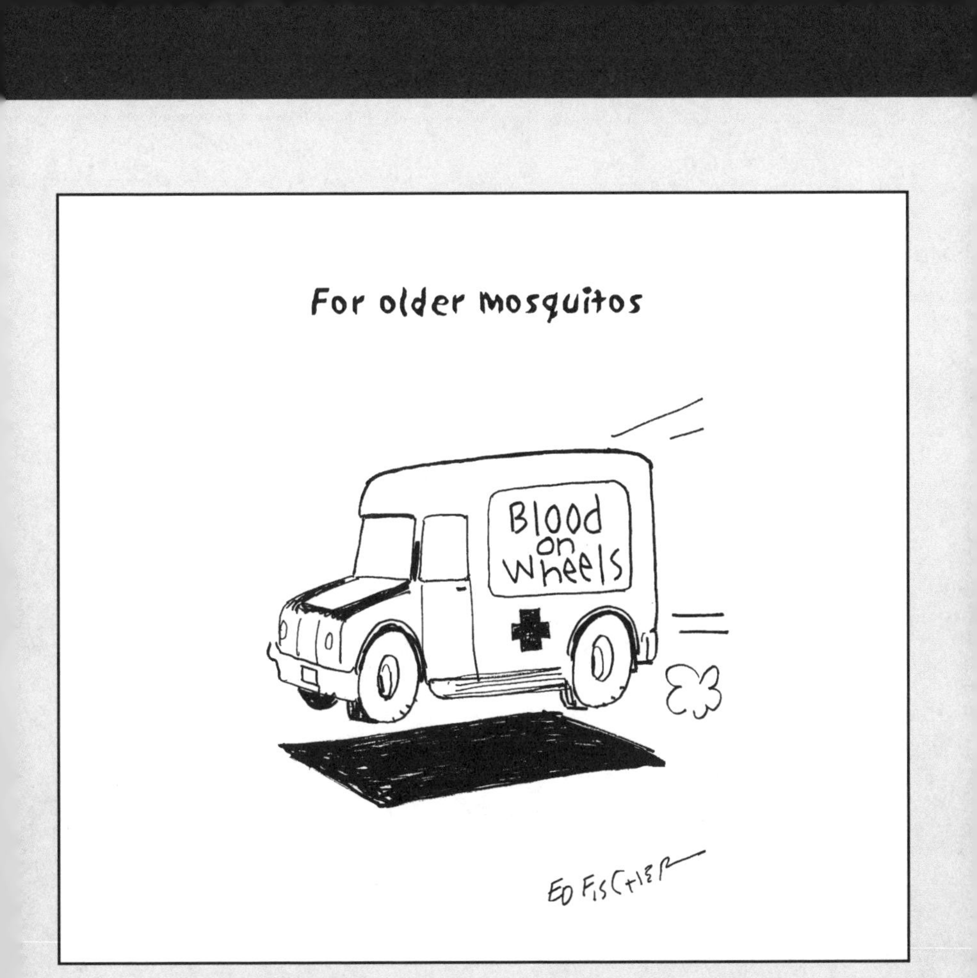
Blood on Wheels
ED FISCHER

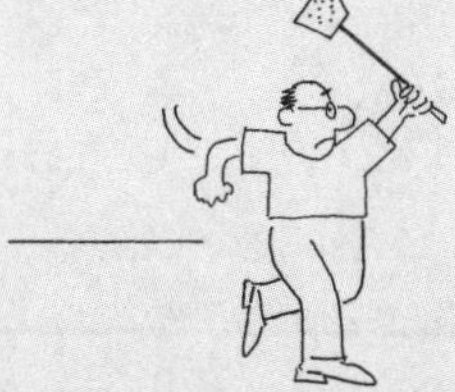

Peace plan

Negotiate with the mosquitos

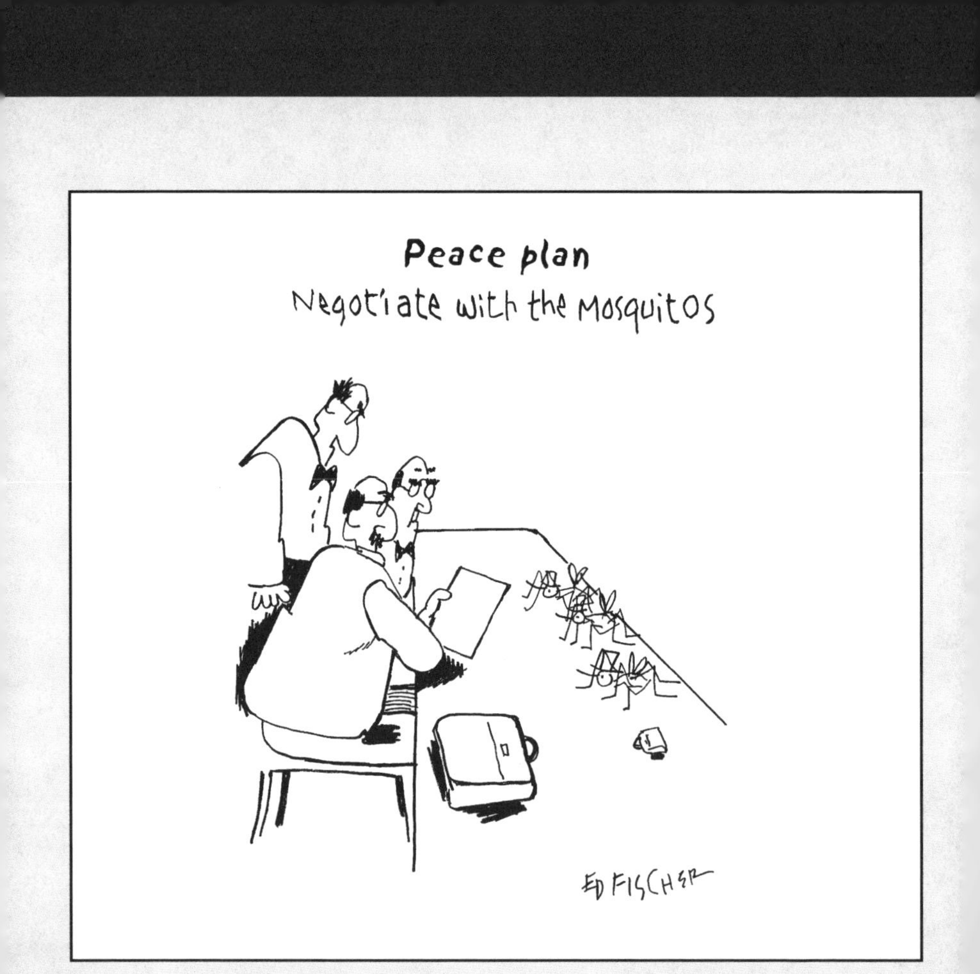
ED FISCHER

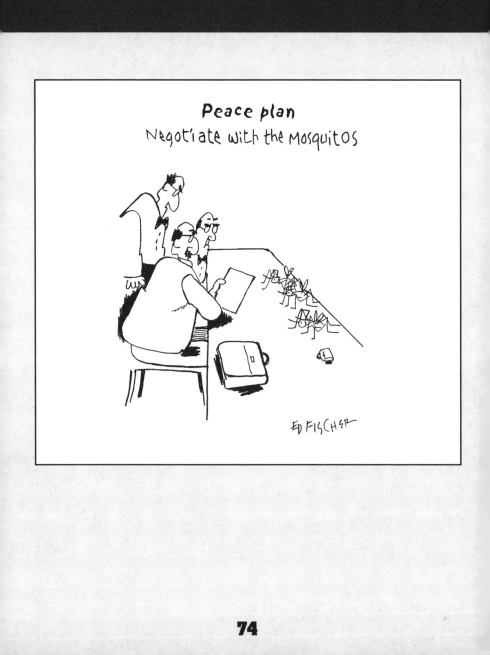

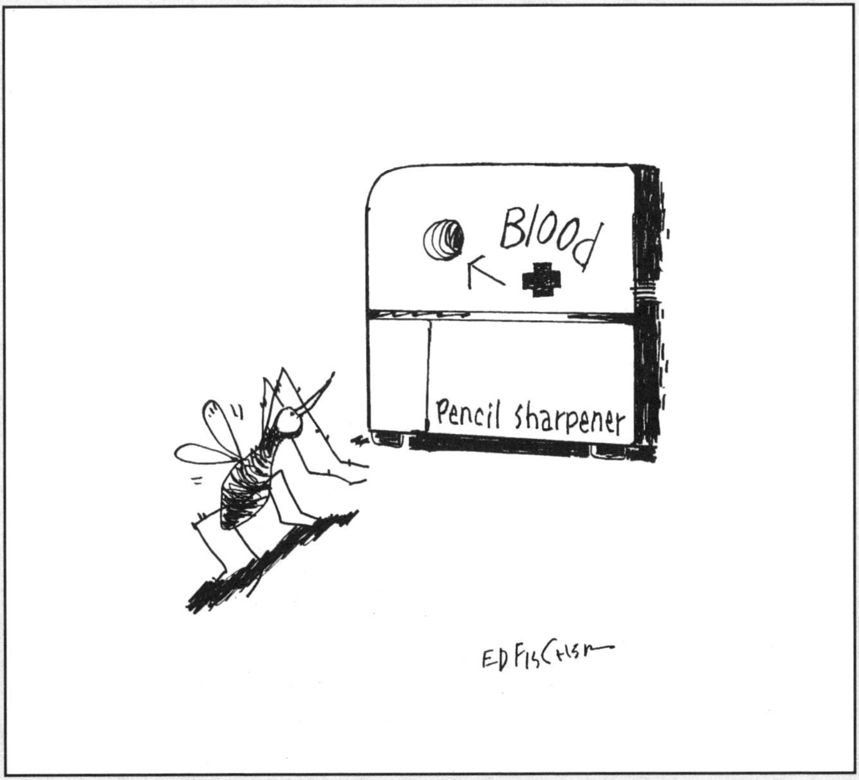
Blood
Pencil sharpener
ED FISCHER

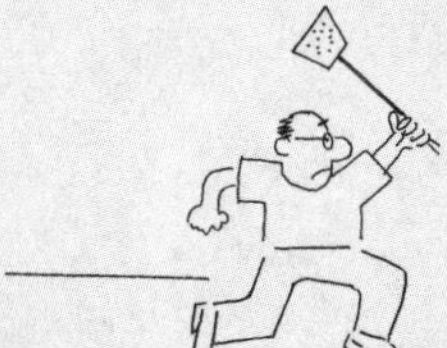

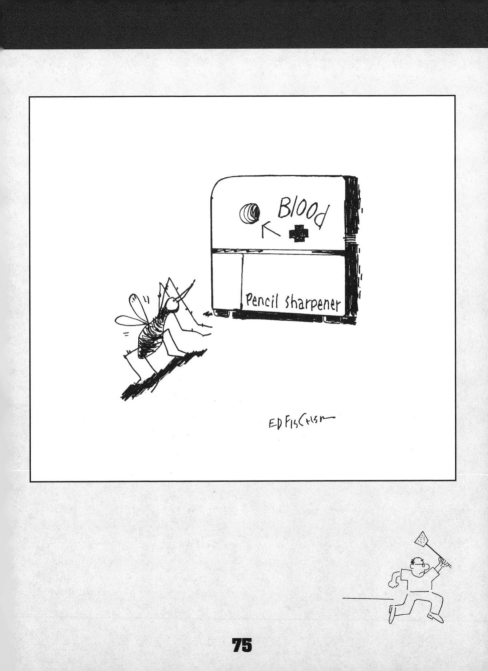

Spray with perfume
(so we can hear and smell them)

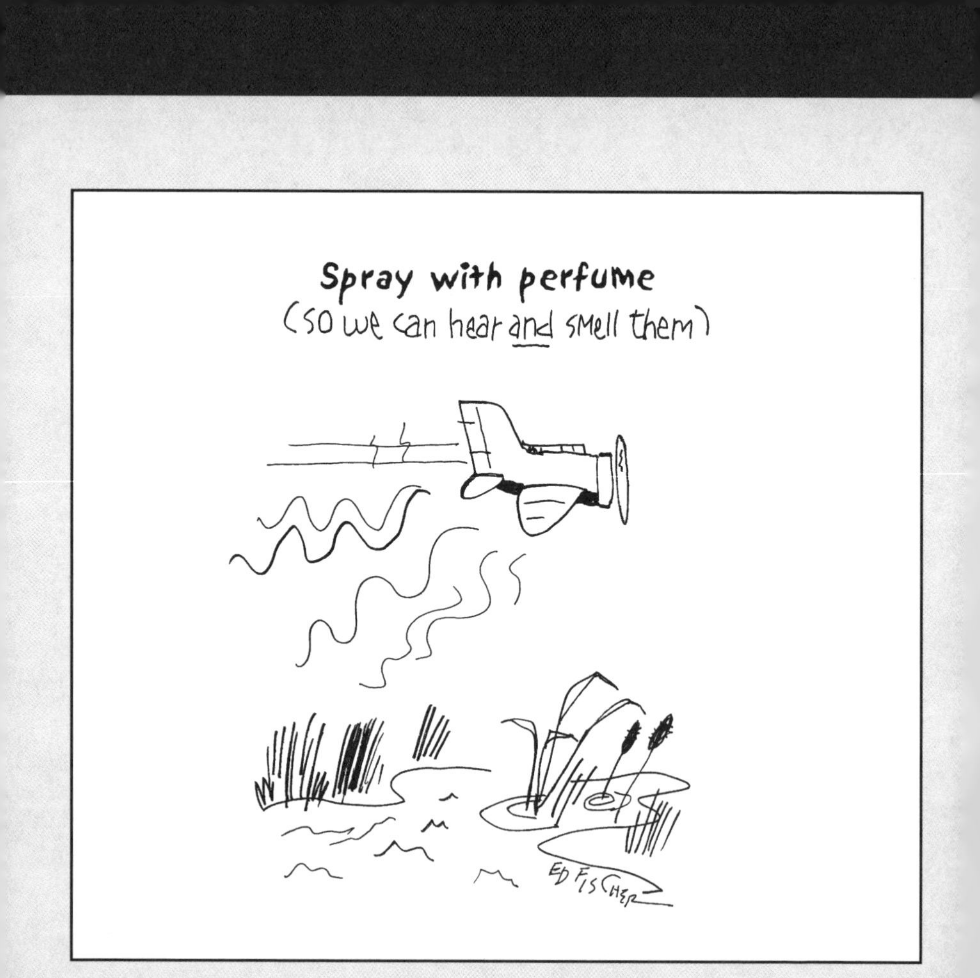
ED FISCHER

Pet mosquito on a leash

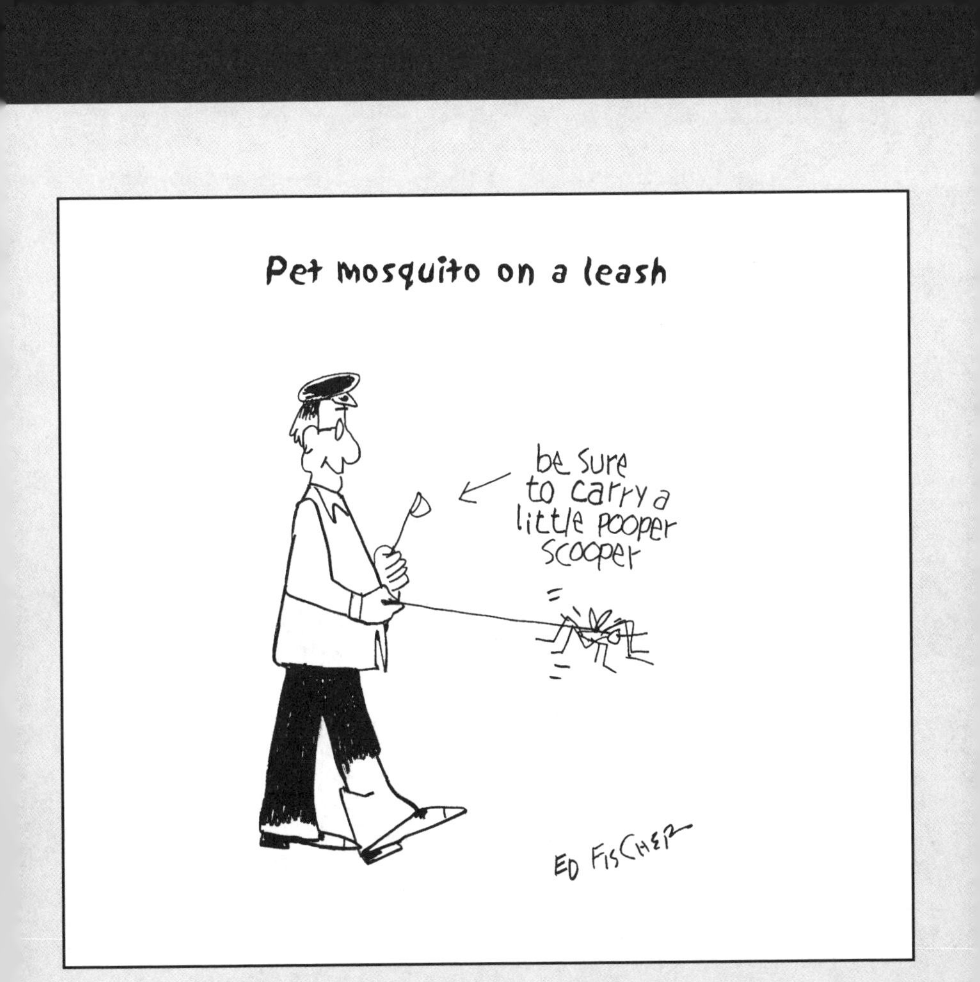
be sure to carry a little pooper scooper
ED FISCHER

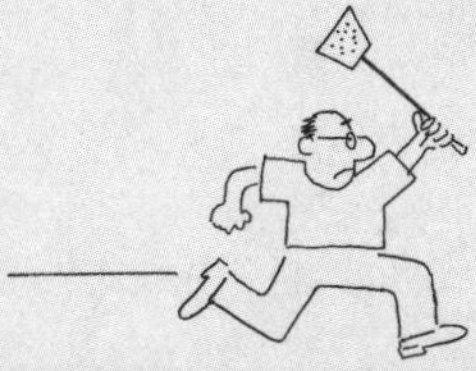

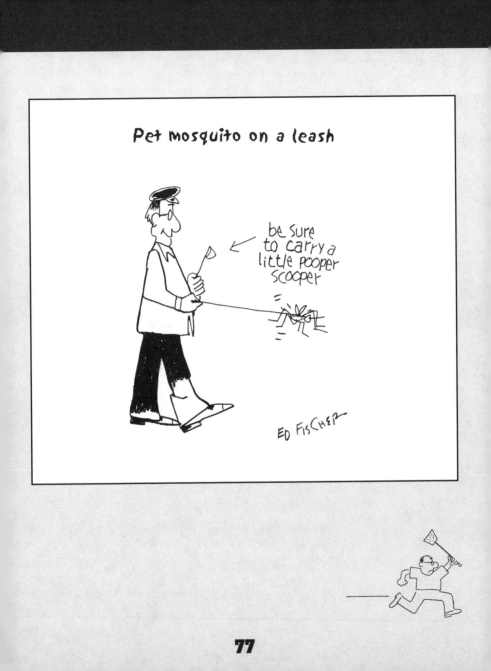

For the Fair

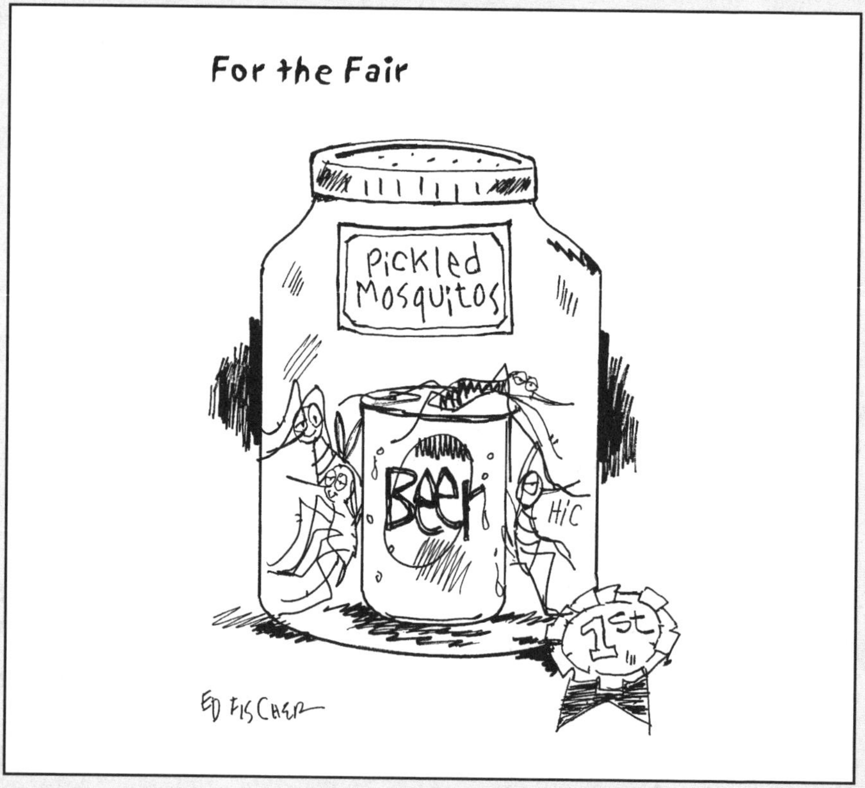
Pickled Mosquitos
Beer
HiC
1st
ED FISCHER

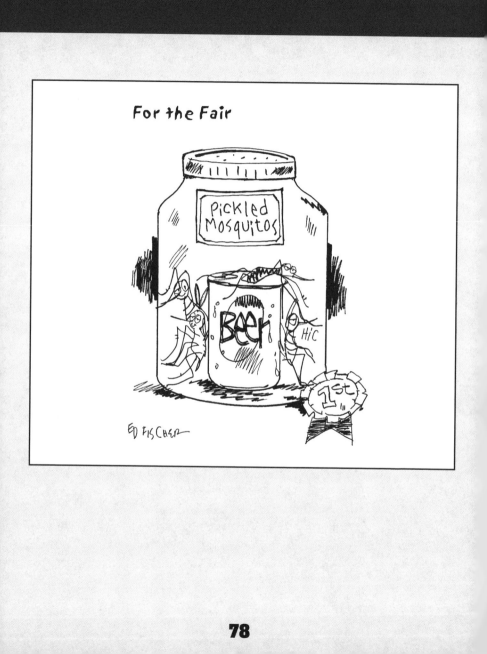

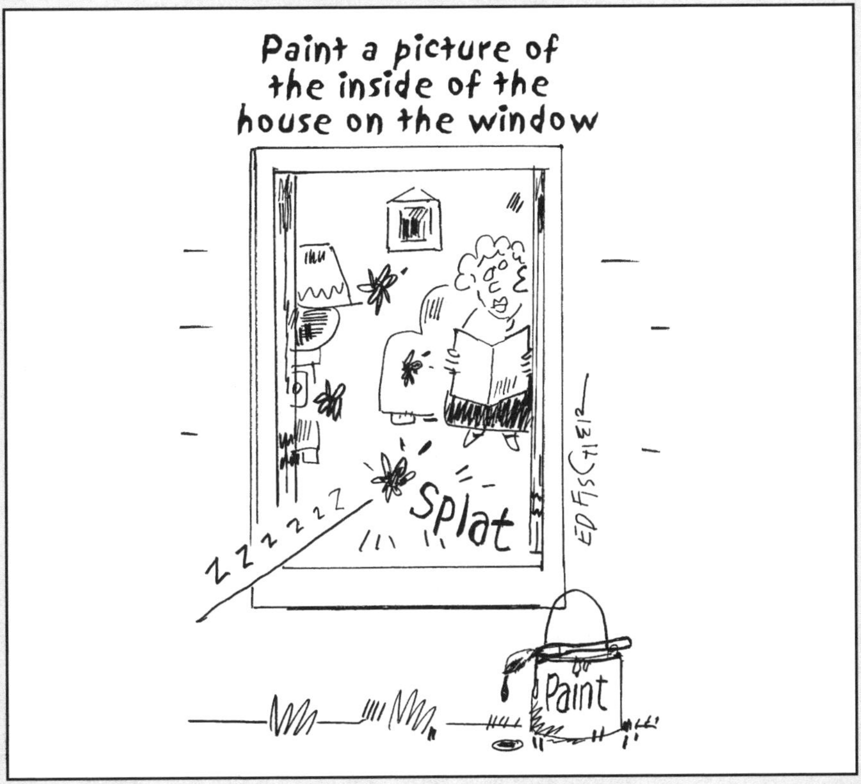
Paint a picture of
the inside of the
house on the window
Splat
Paint

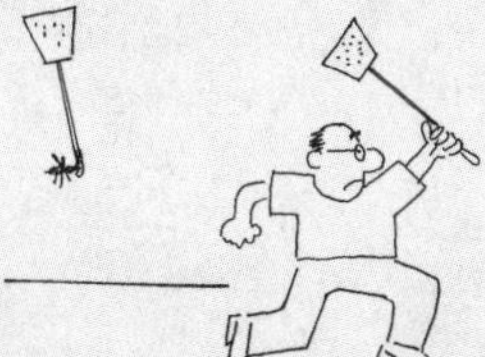

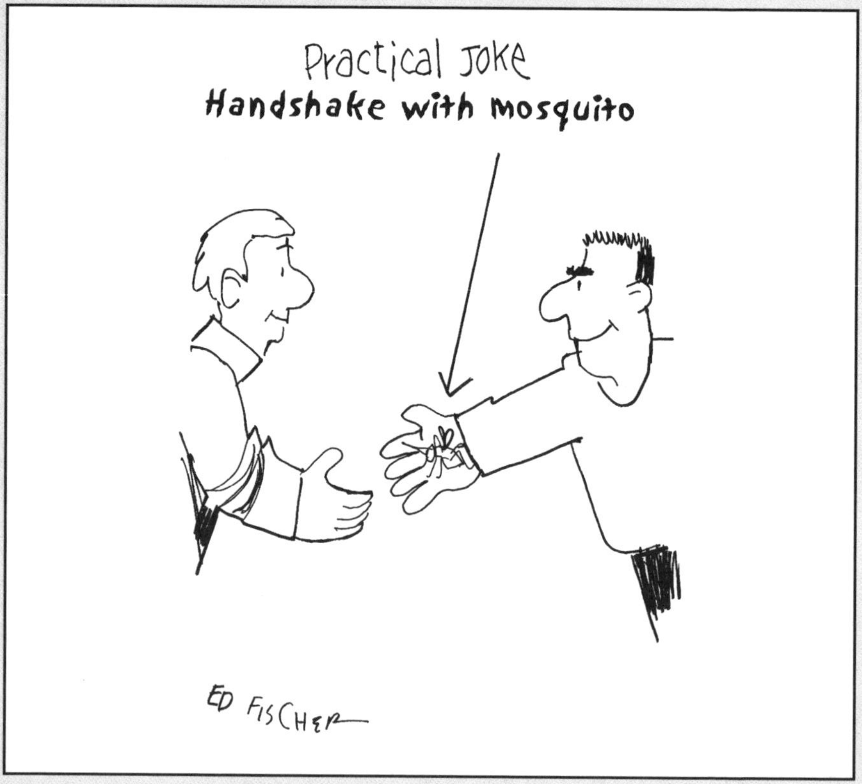
Practical Joke
Handshake with mosquito
ED FISCHER

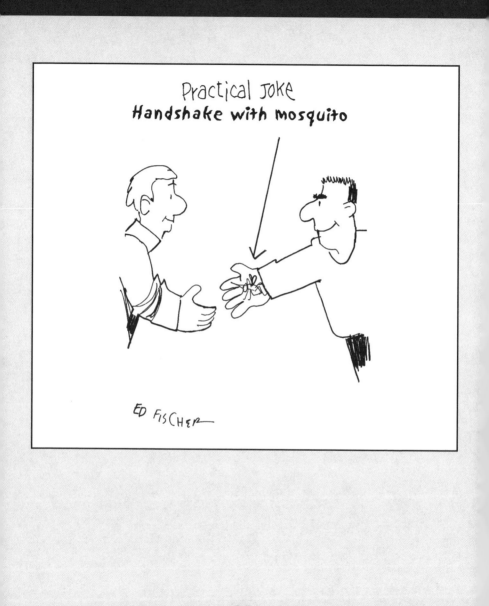

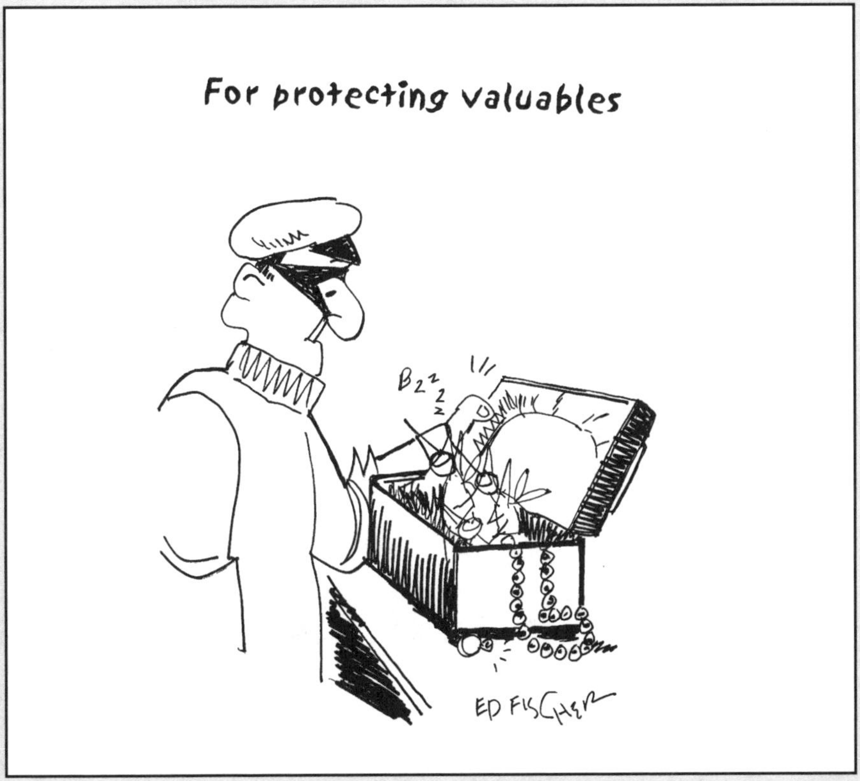
For protecting valuables
Bzzz
ED FISCHER

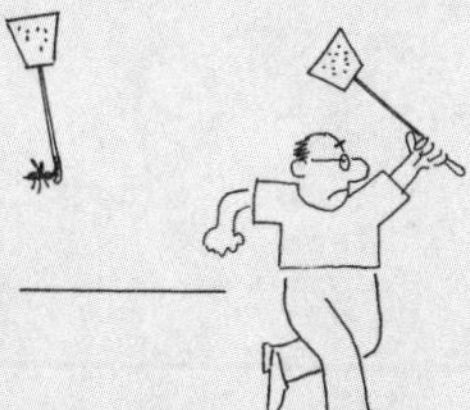

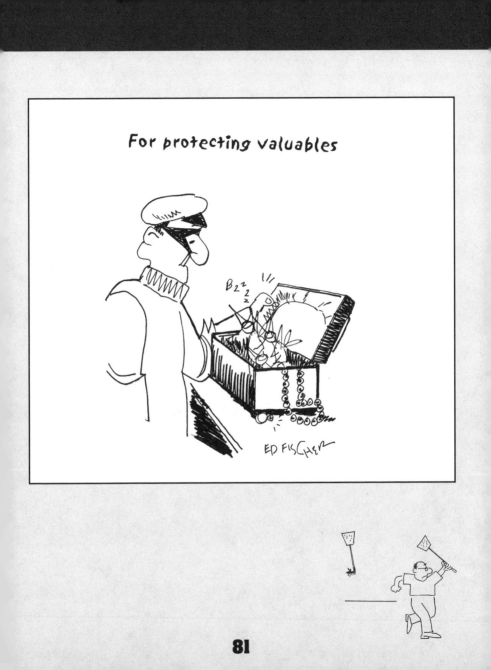

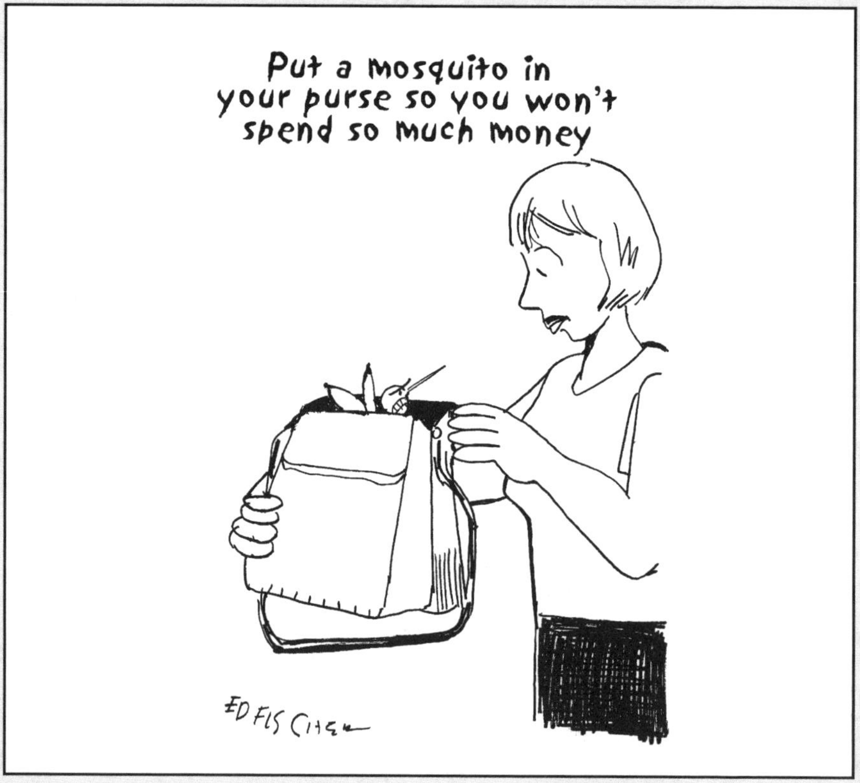
Put a mosquito in
your purse so you won't
spend so much money

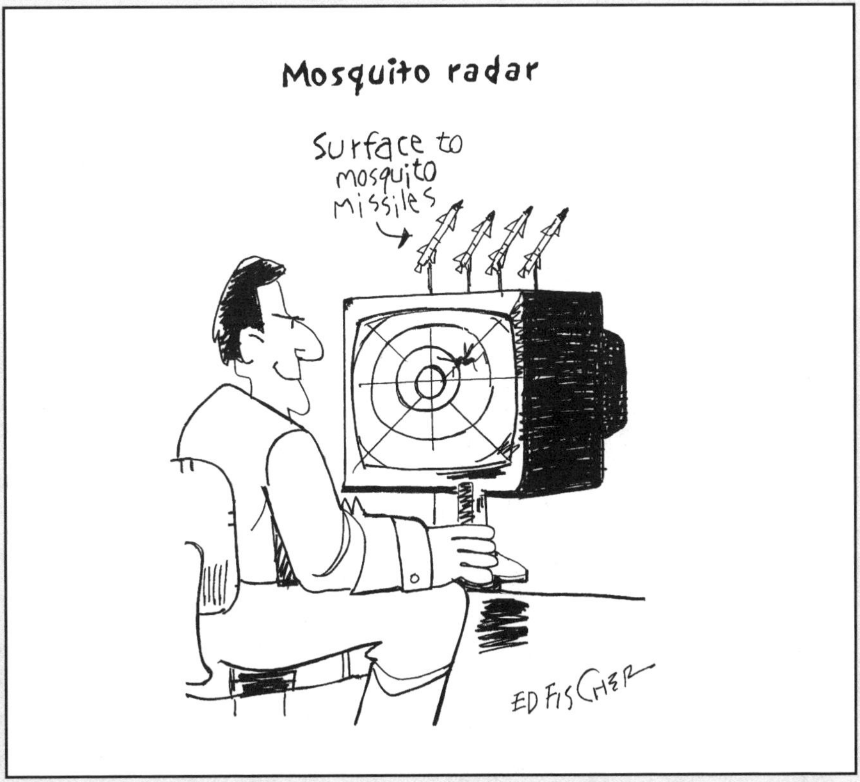
Mosquito radar
Surface to mosquito missiles
ED FISCHER

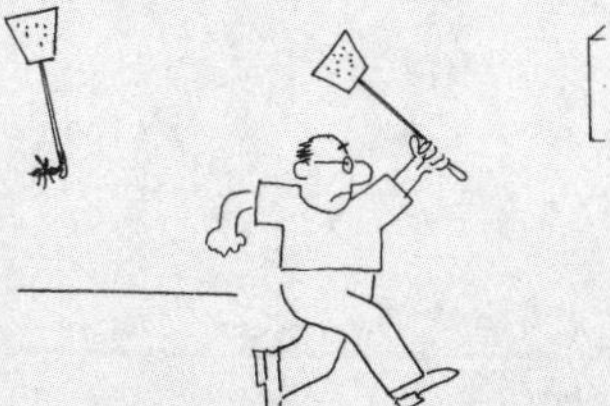

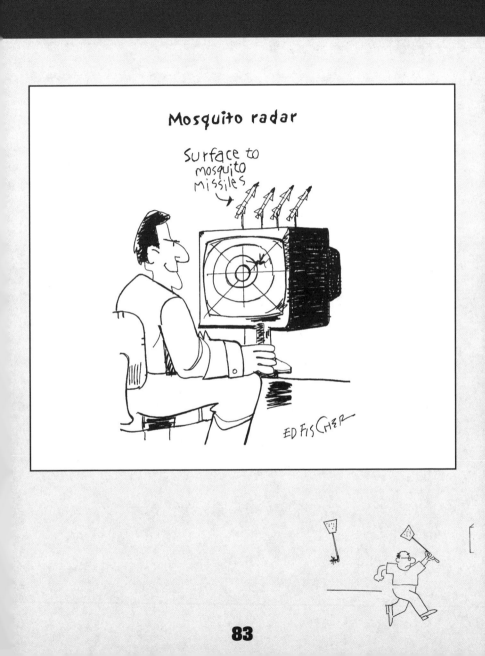

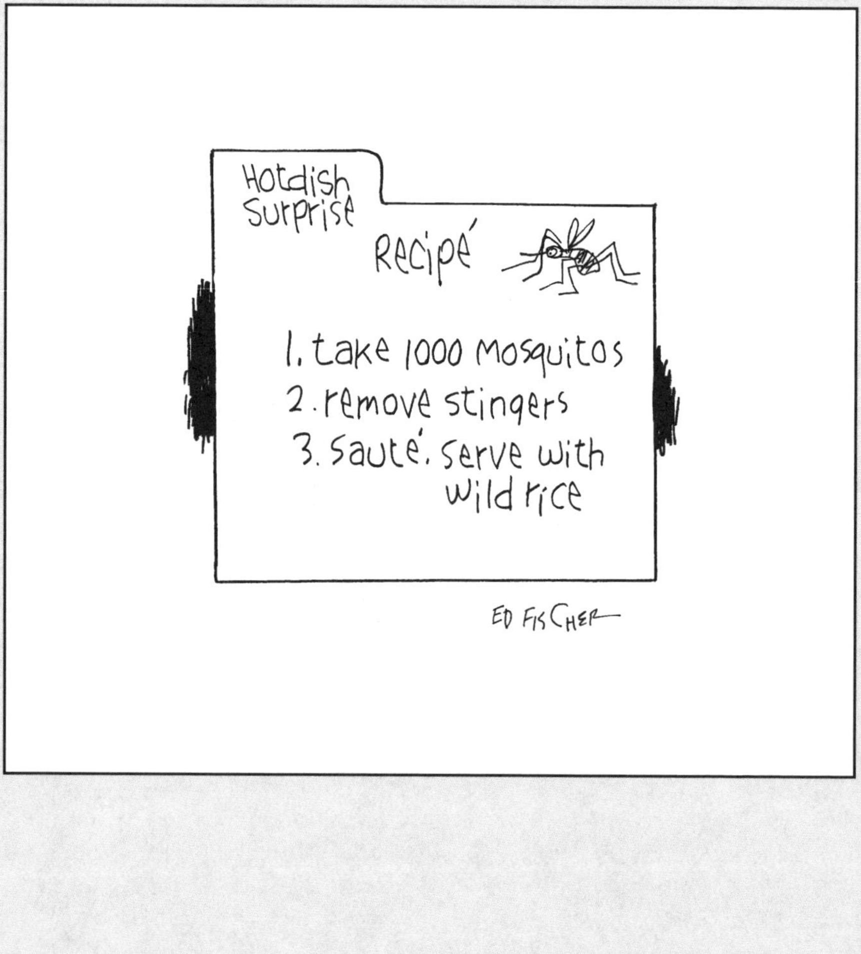
Hotdish Surprise
Recipé
1. take 1000 mosquitos
2. remove stingers
3. sauté. serve with wild rice
ED FISCHER

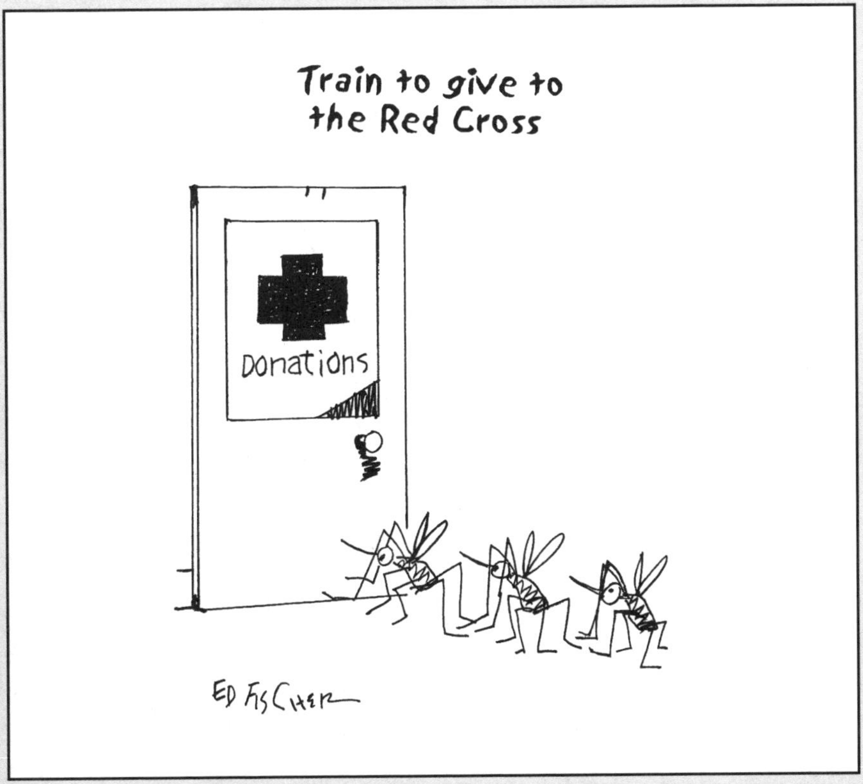
Donations
ED FISCHER

Train to give to the Red Cross

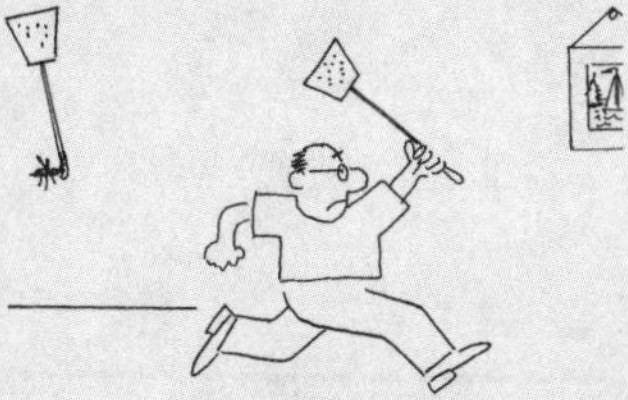

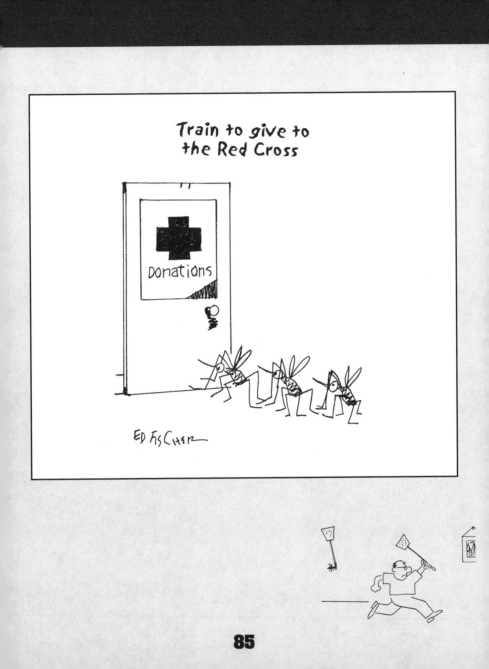

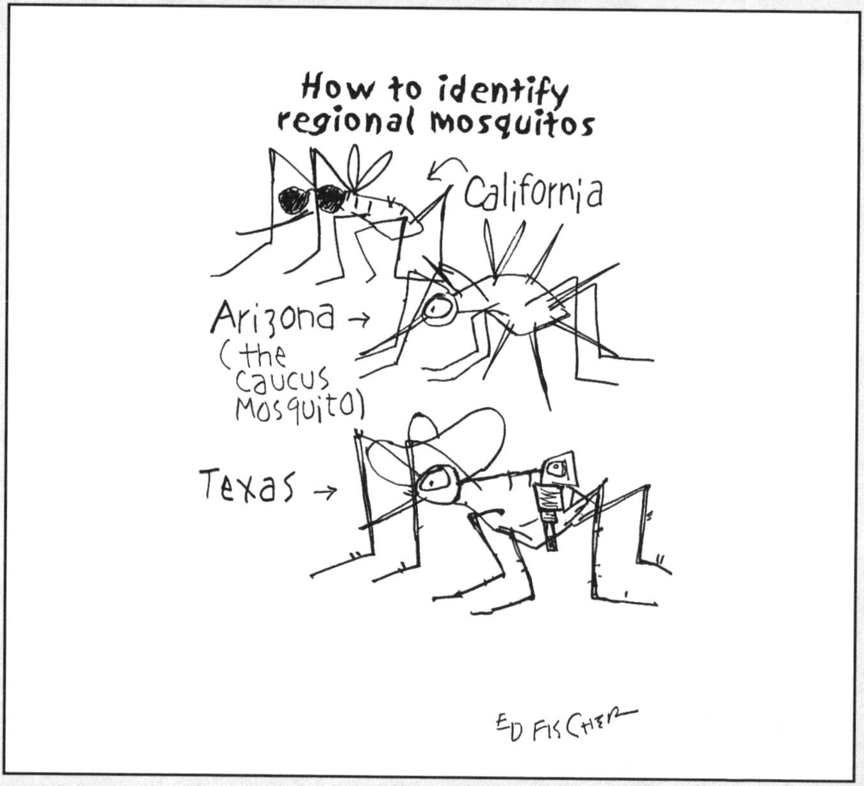
How to identify regional mosquitos
California
Arizona →
(the caucus mosquito)
Texas →
ED FISCHER

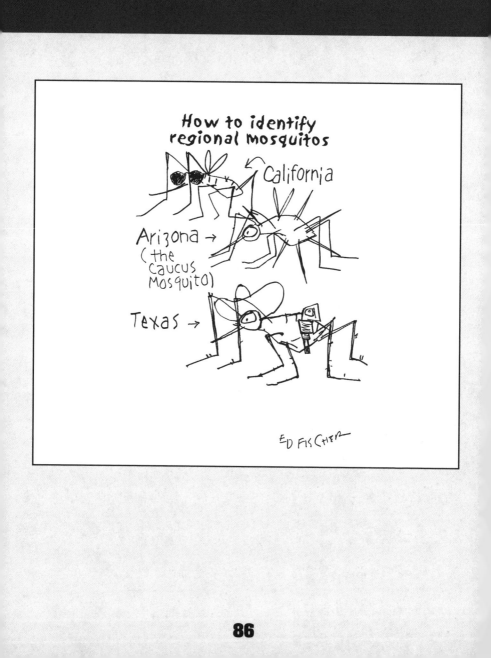

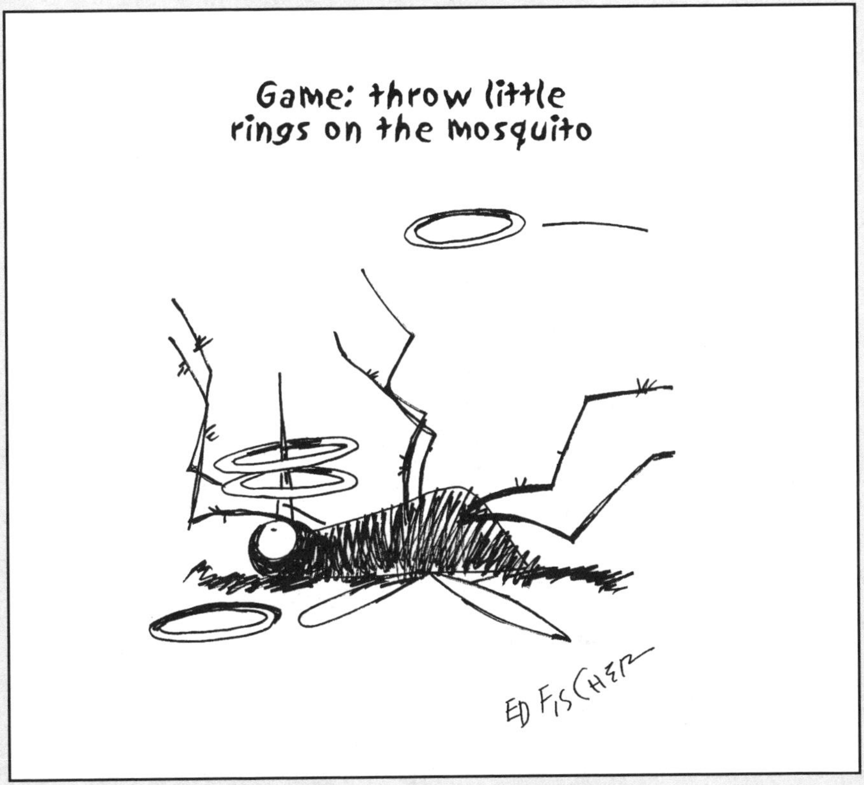
Game: throw little rings on the mosquito
ED FISCHER

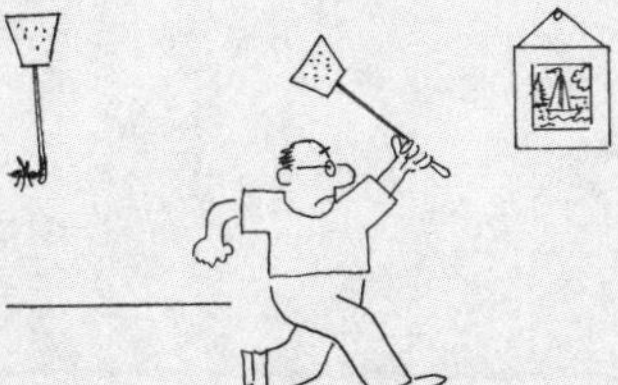

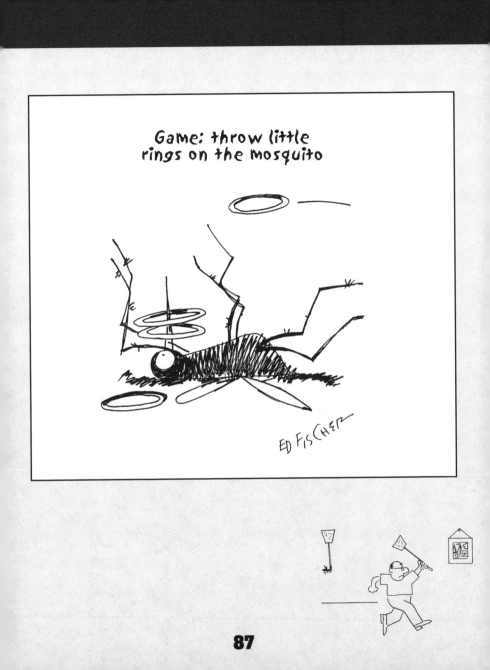

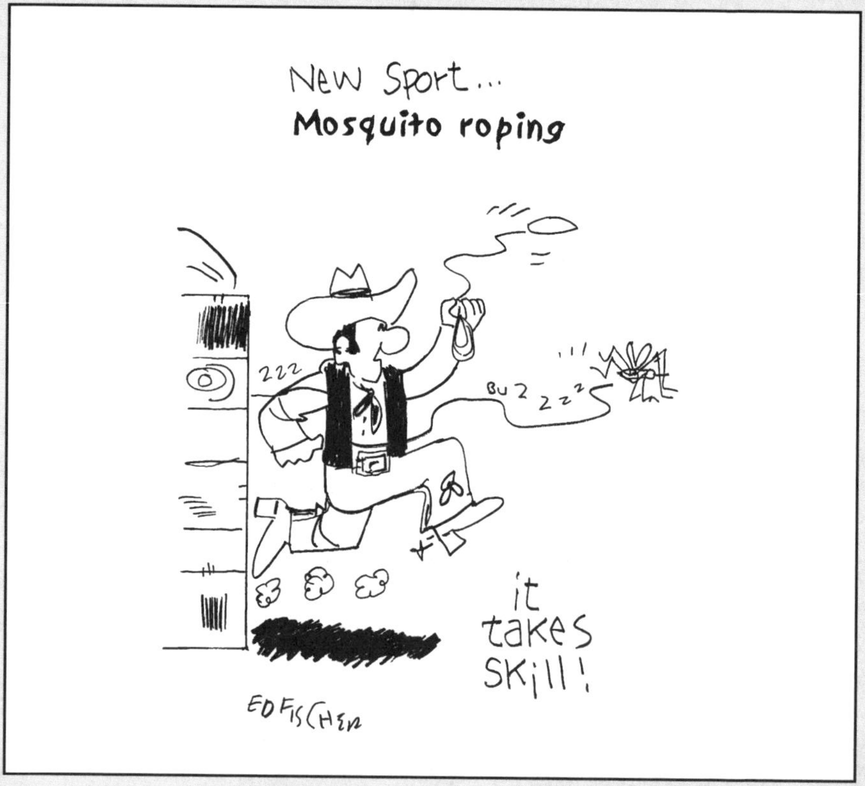
New Sport...
Mosquito roping
zzz
BUZZZZ
it takes skill!
ED FISCHER

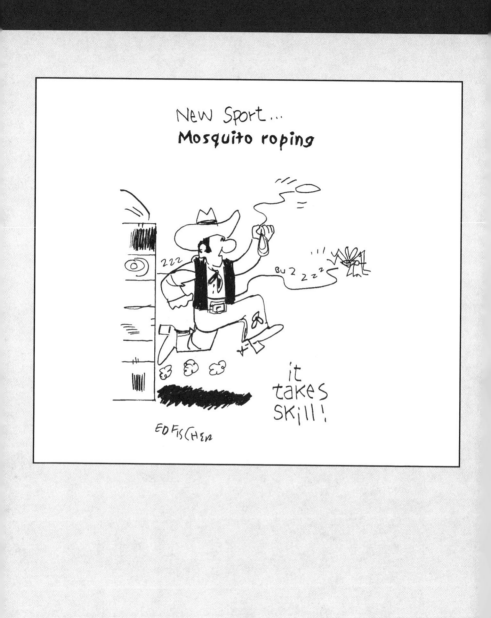

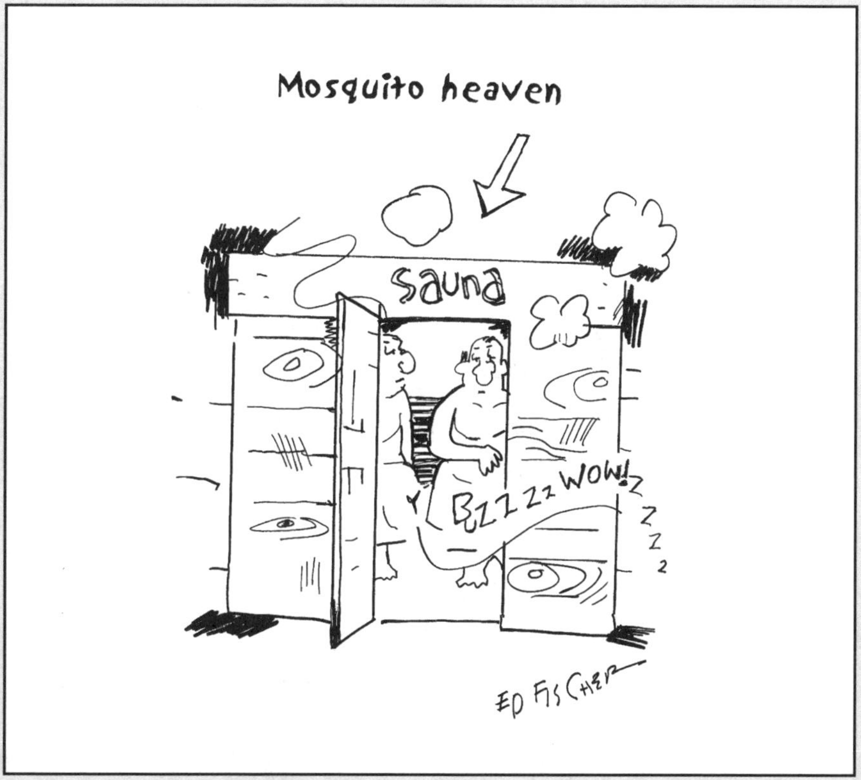
Mosquito heaven
Sauna
BUZZZzz WOW!
Zzzz
ED FISCHER

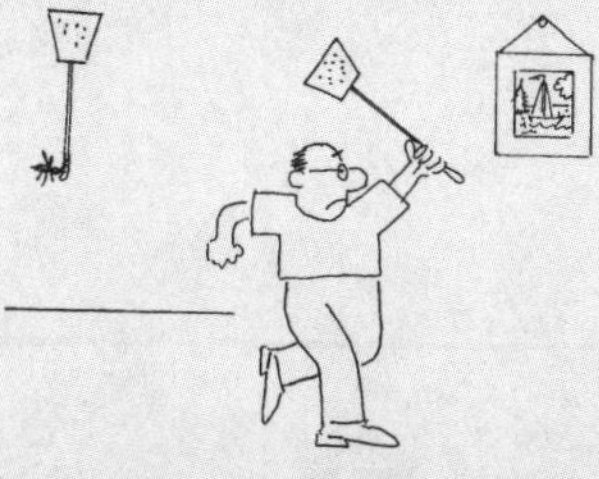

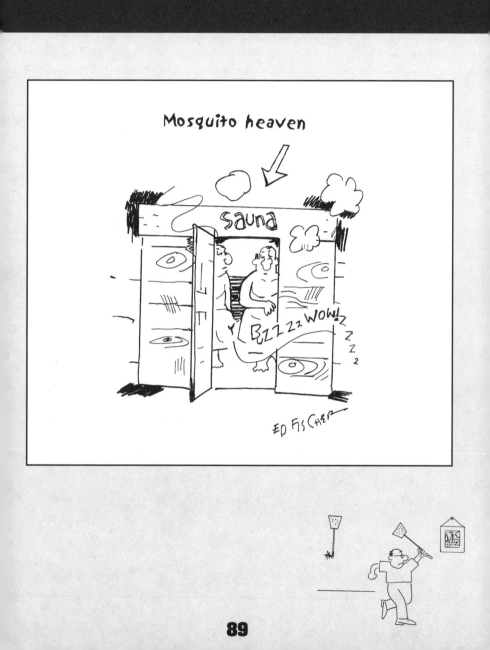

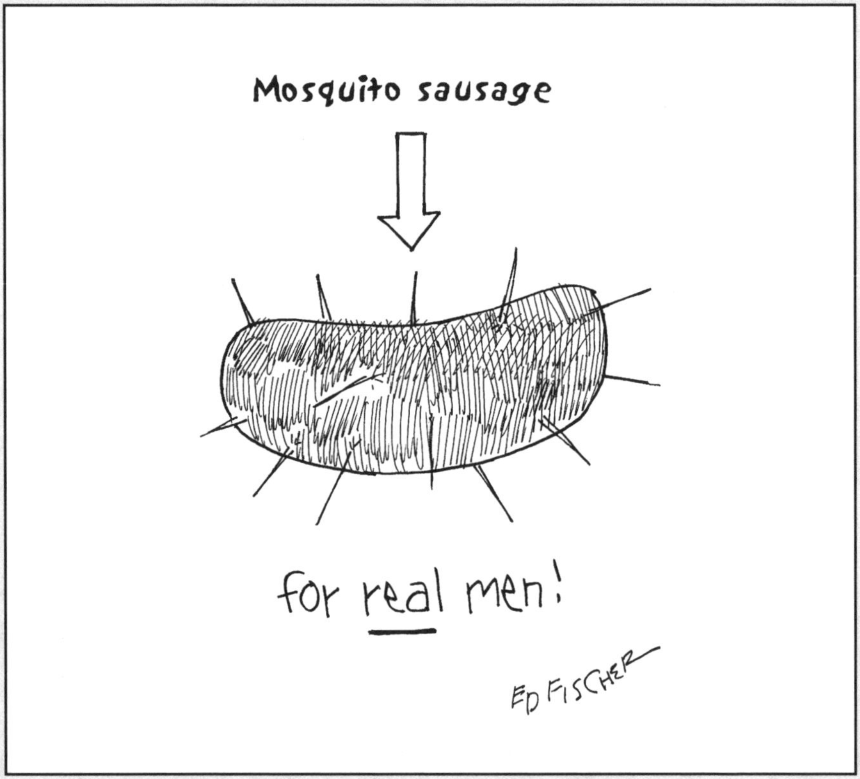
Mosquito sausage
for real men!
ED FISCHER

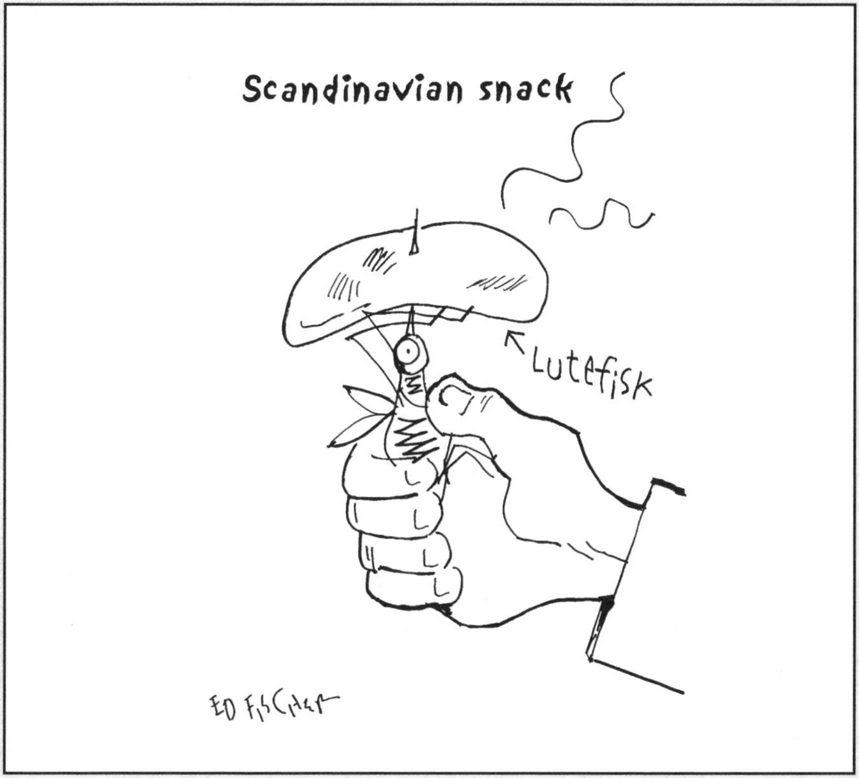
Scandinavian snack
Lutefisk
ED FISCHER

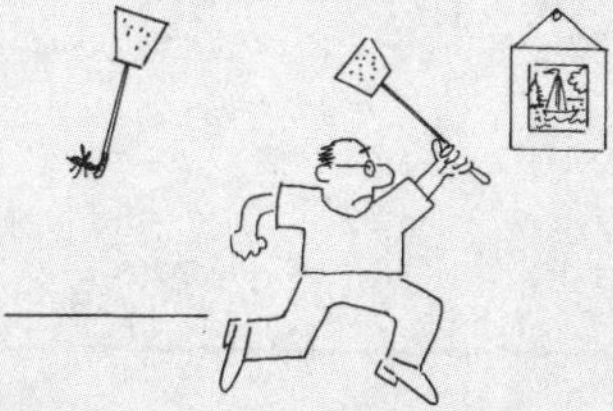

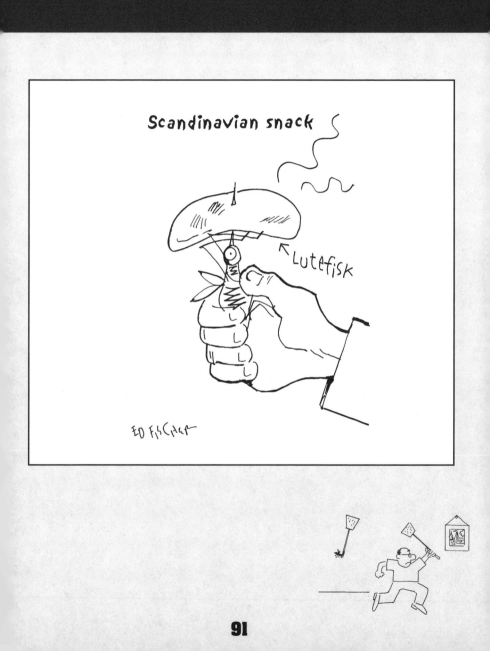

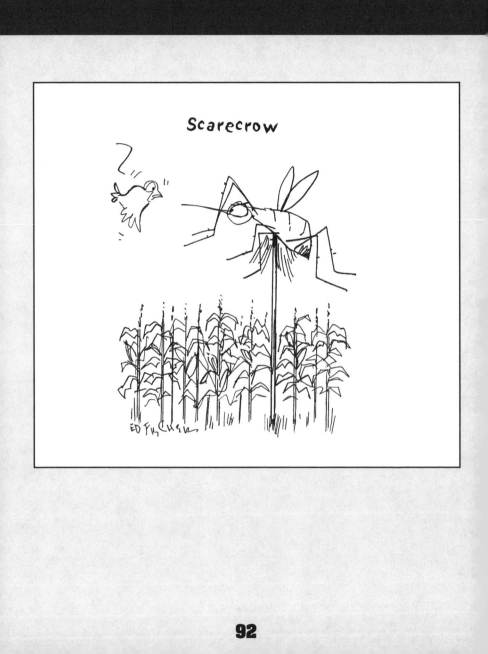

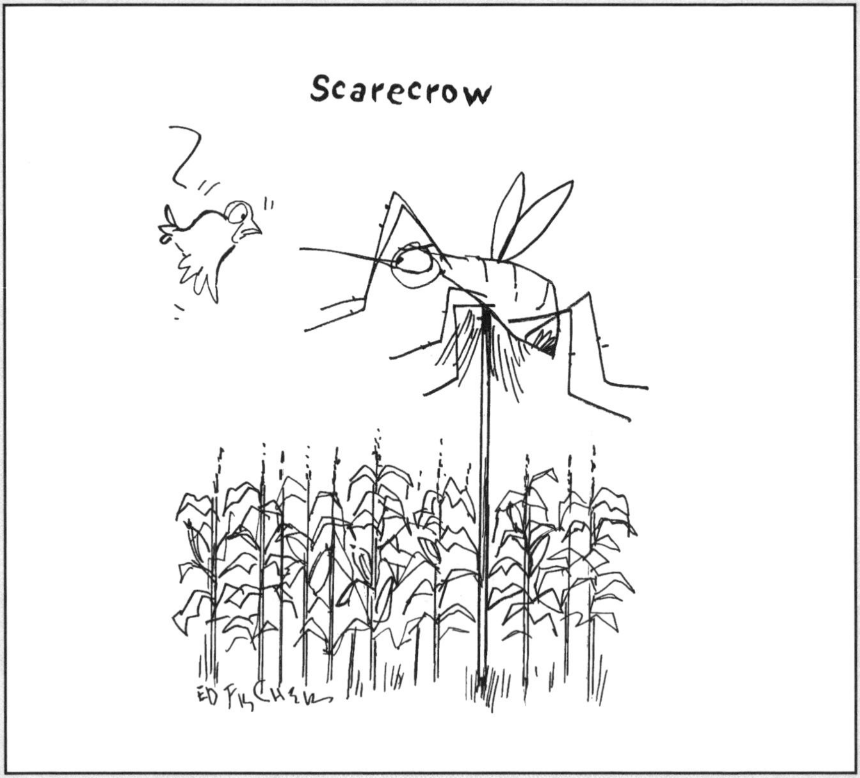
Scarecrow
ED FISCHER

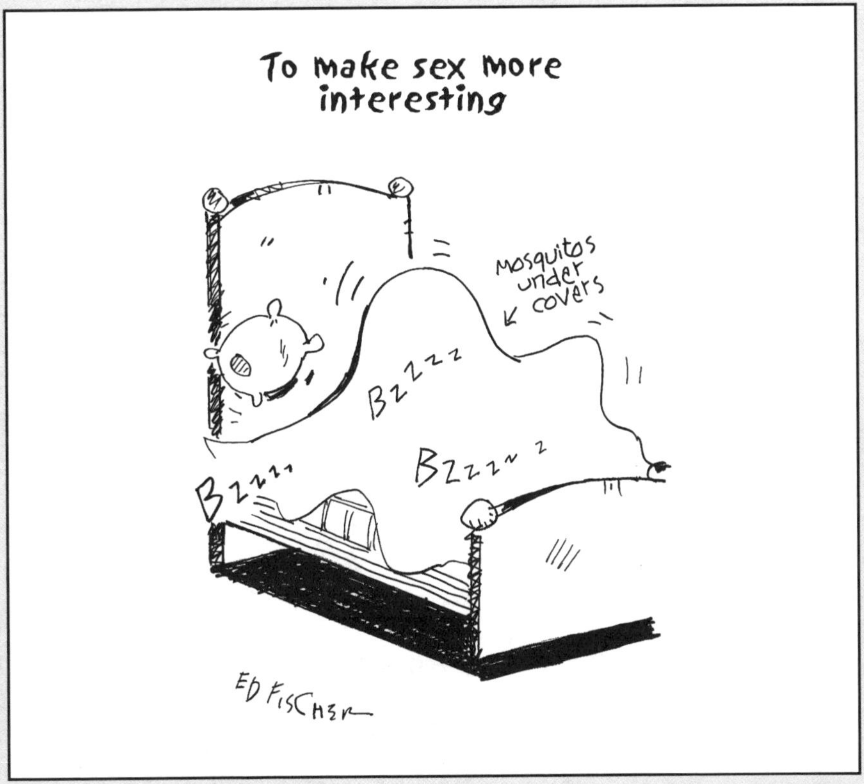
To make sex more interesting
Mosquitos under covers
Bzzzz
Bzzzz z
Bzzzz
ED FISCHER

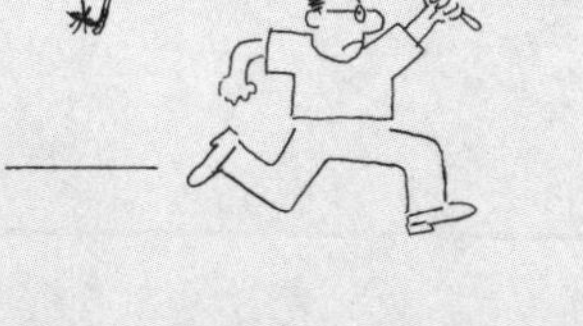

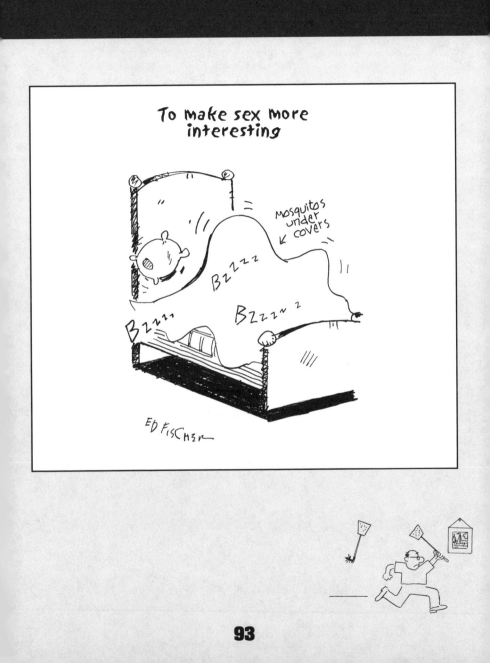

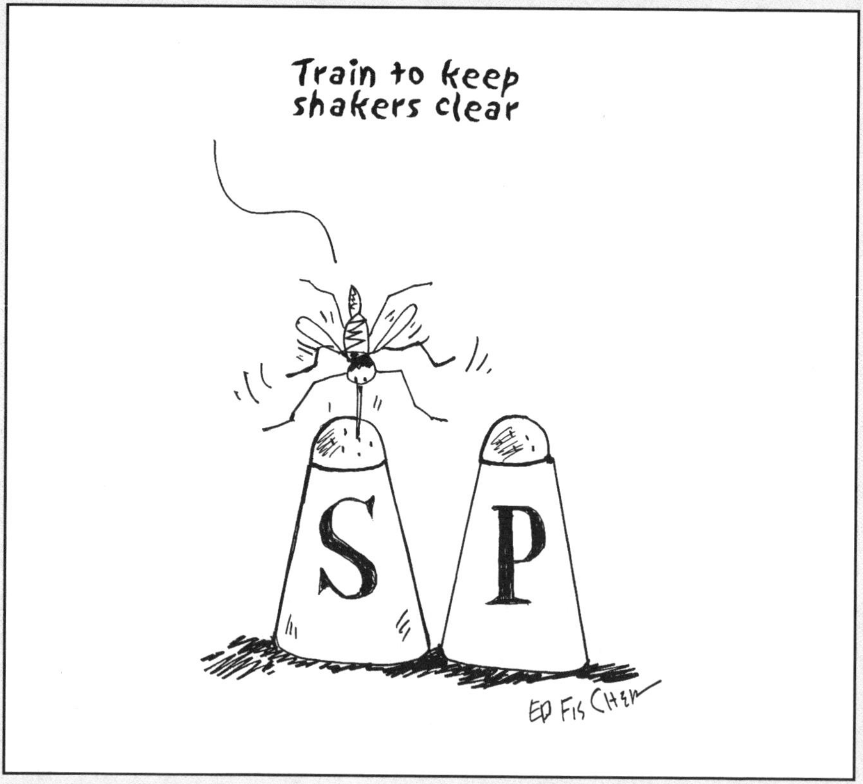
Train to keep
shakers clear
S
P
ED FISCHER

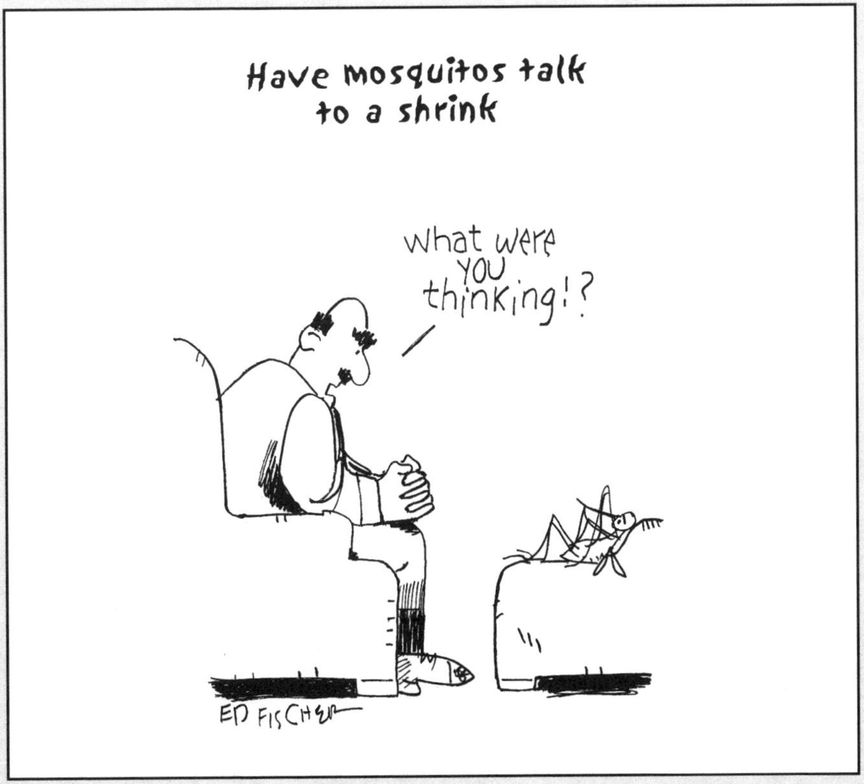
Have mosquitos talk to a shrink
what were YOU thinking!?
ED FISCHER

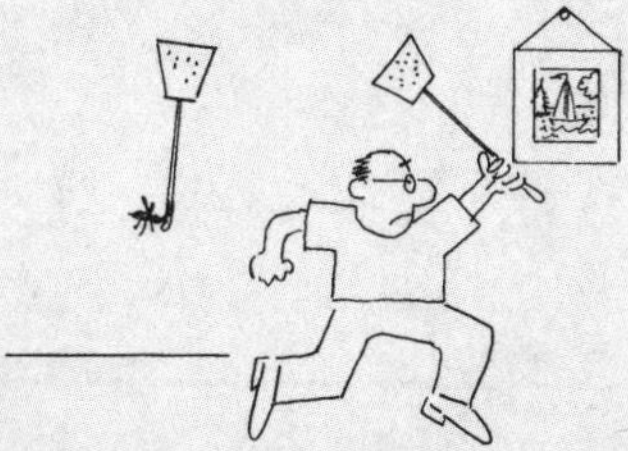

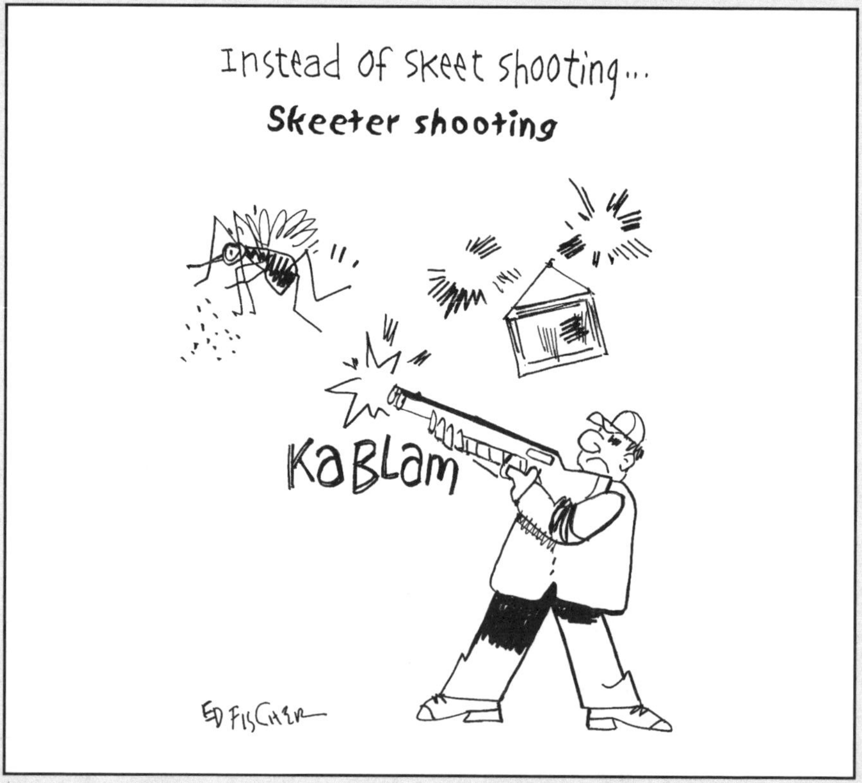
Instead of skeet shooting...
Skeeter shooting
KaBLam
ED FISCHER

Sting operation

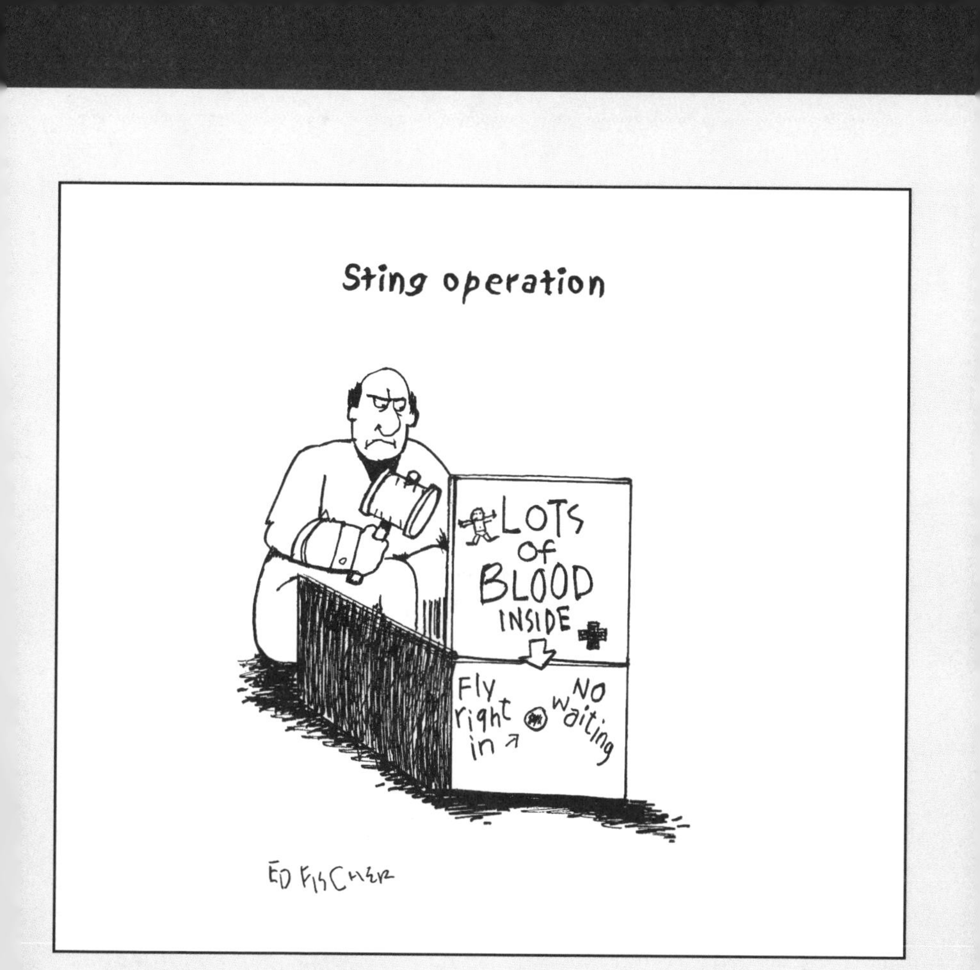
LOTS of BLOOD INSIDE
Fly right in
NO waiting
ED FISCHER

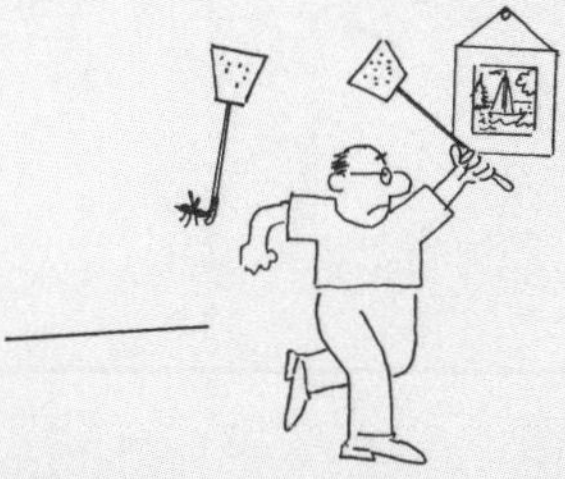

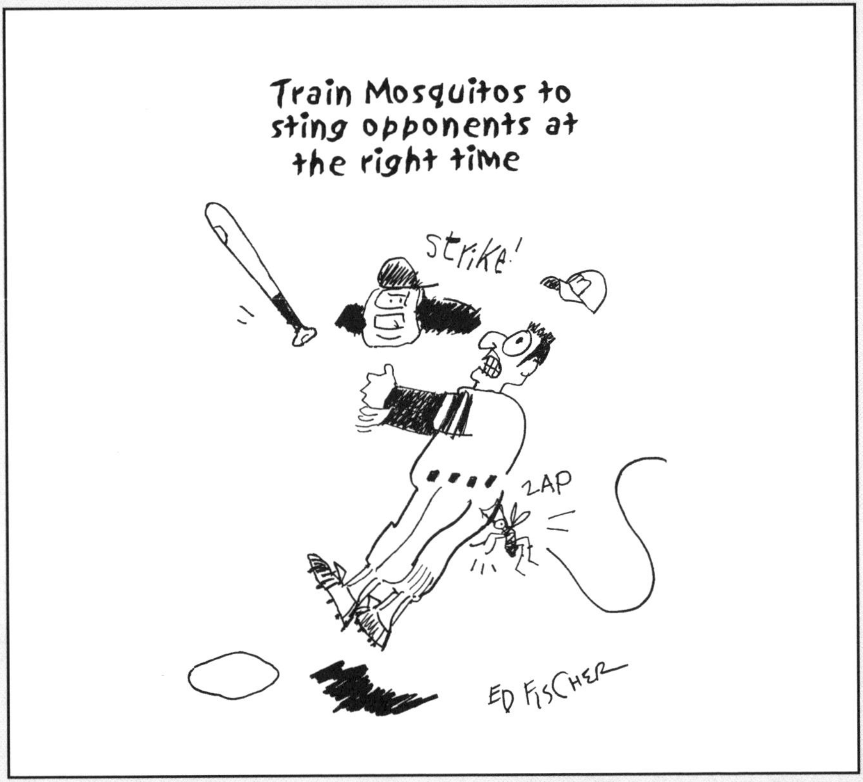
Train Mosquitos to
sting opponents at
the right time
strike!
ZAP
ED FISCHER

A more potent 'Stinger' alcoholic drink

ED FISCHER

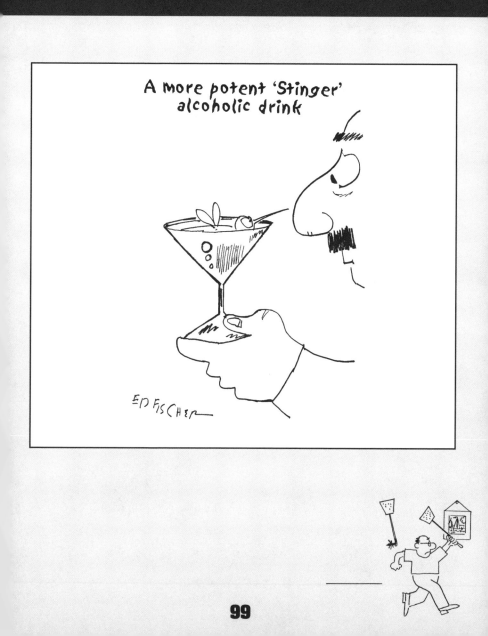

Use as tacks

Bulletin Board
ED FISCHER

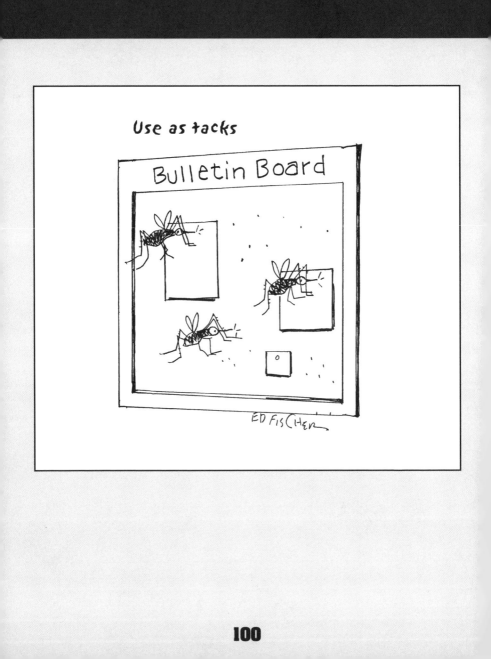

Get them their own tent

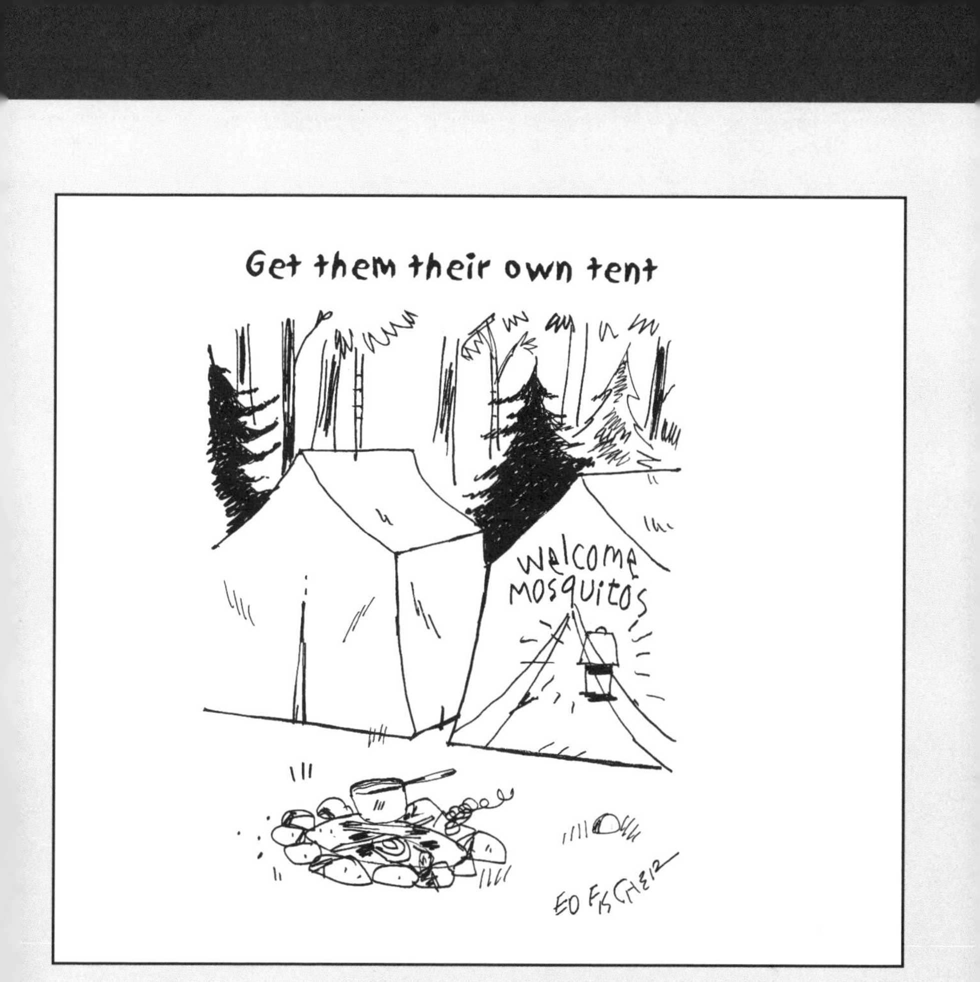
welcome
MOSQUITOS
ED FISCHER

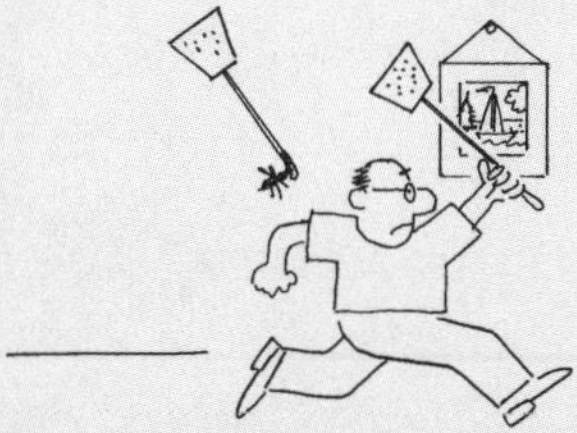

Develop mosquitos that tickle rather than sting

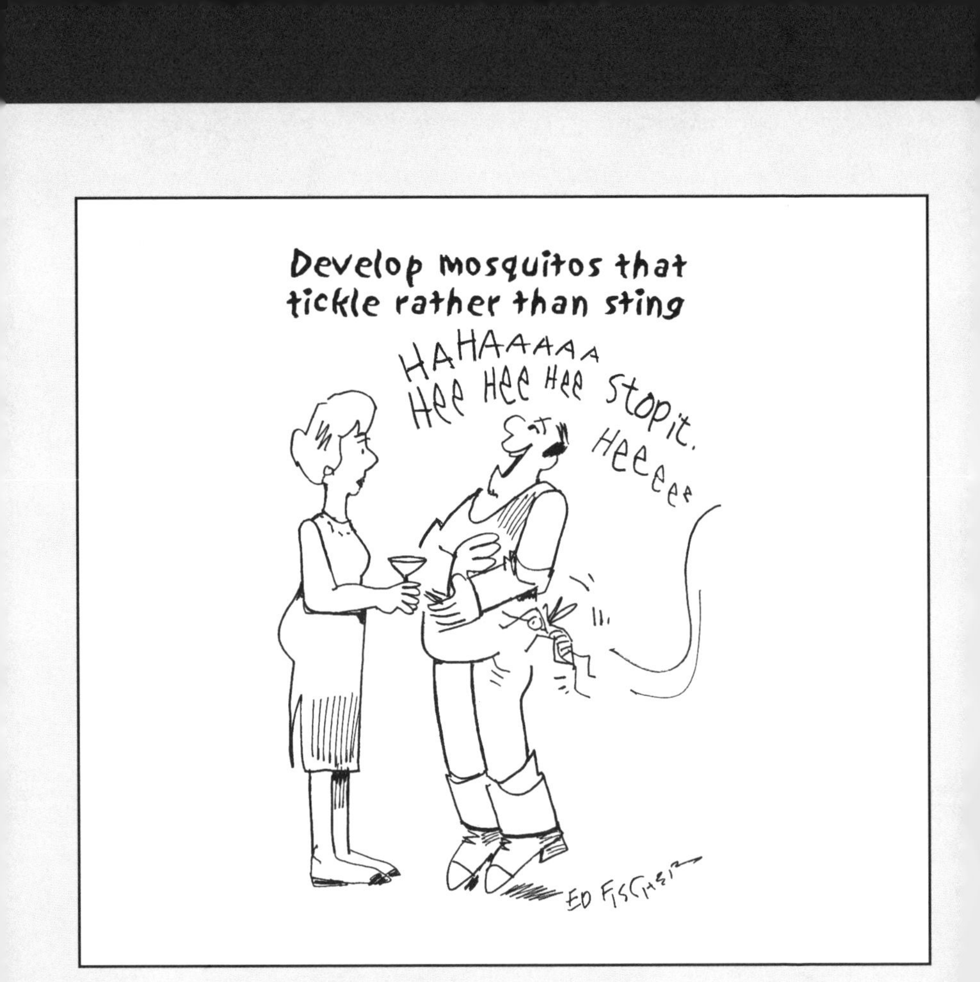
HAHAAAAA
Hee Hee Hee
Stop it.
Heeeee
ED FISCHER

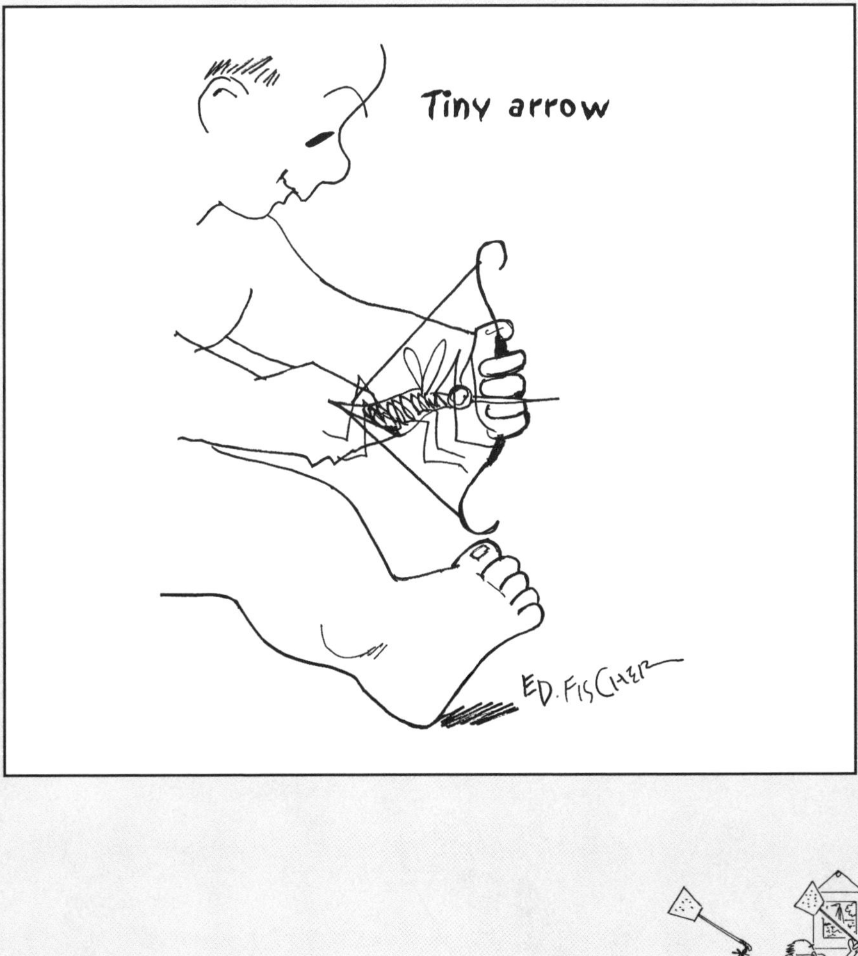
Tiny arrow
ED. FISCHER

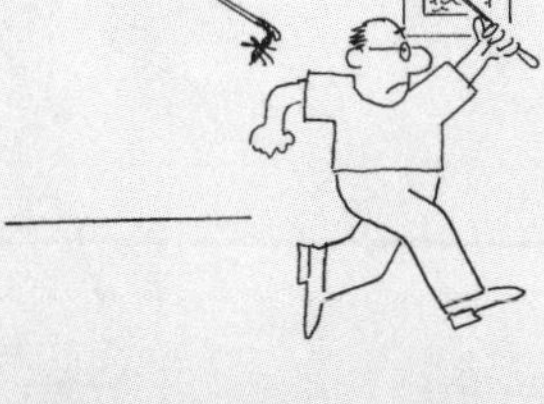

Live toothpicks

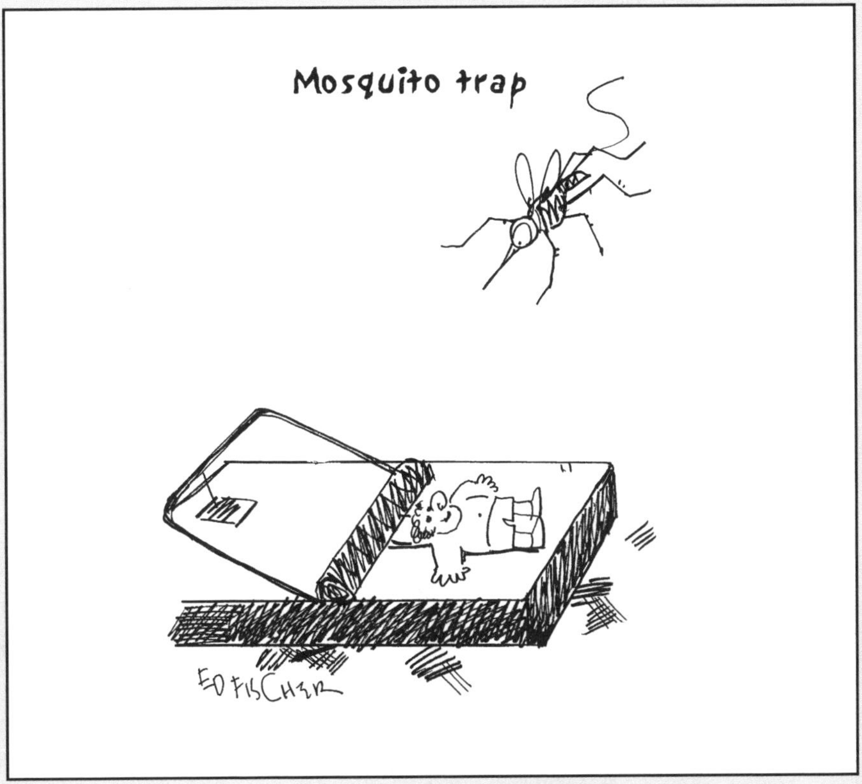
Mosquito trap
ED FISCHER

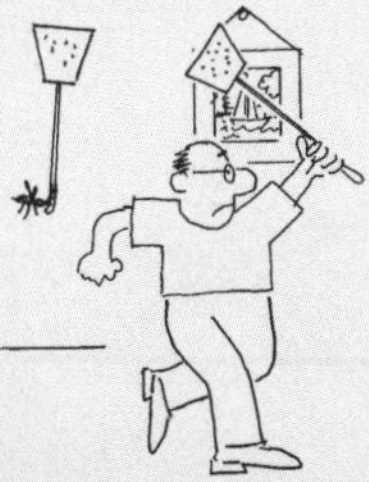

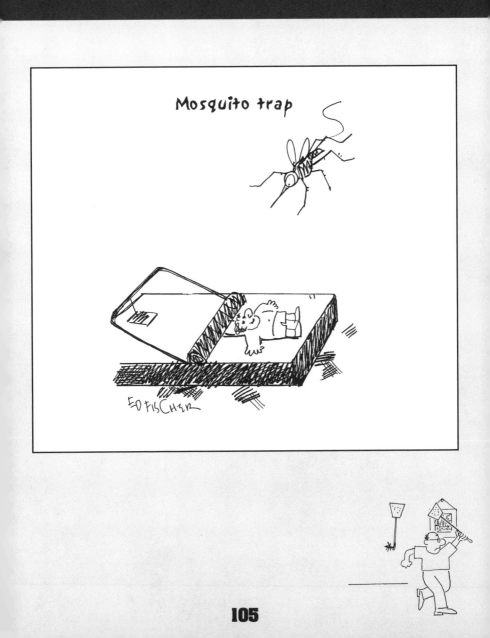

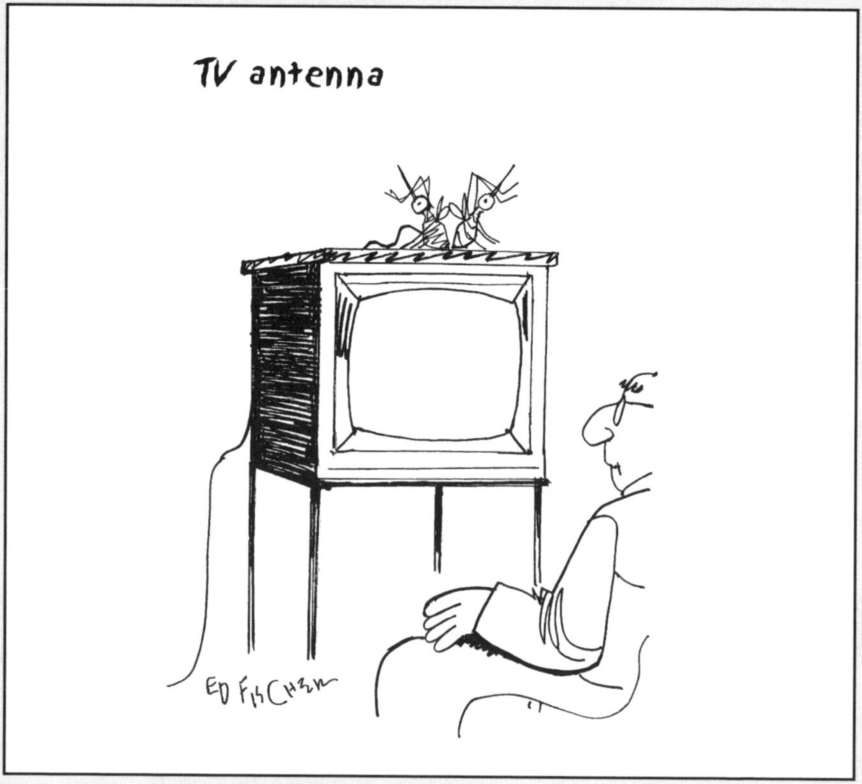
TV antenna
ED FISCHER

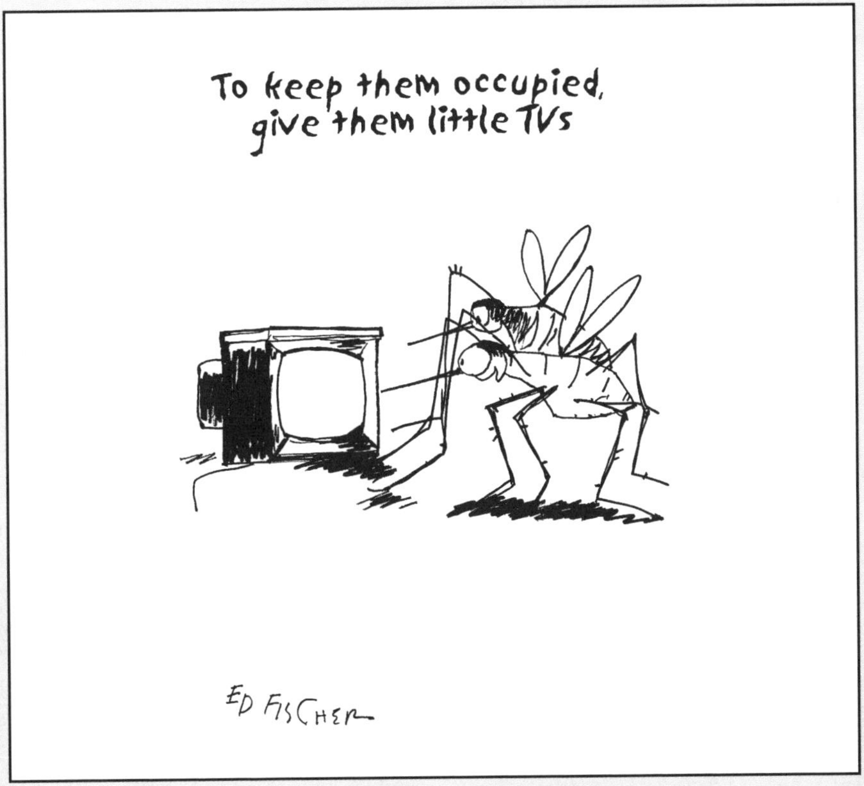
To keep them occupied,
give them little TVs
ED FISCHER

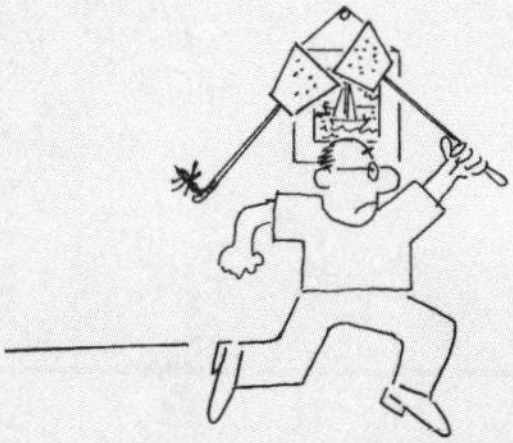

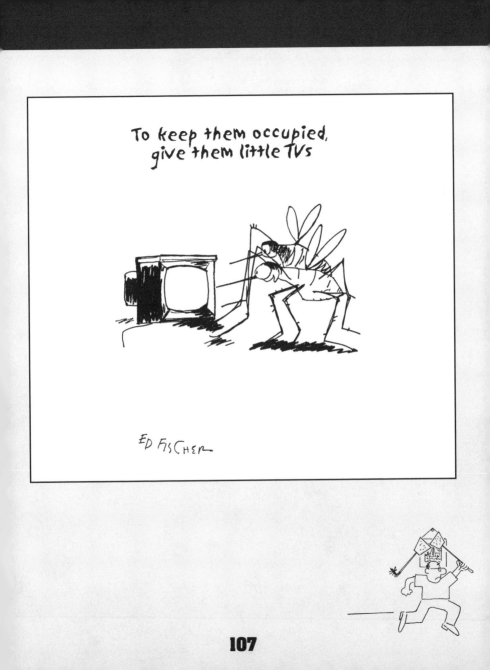

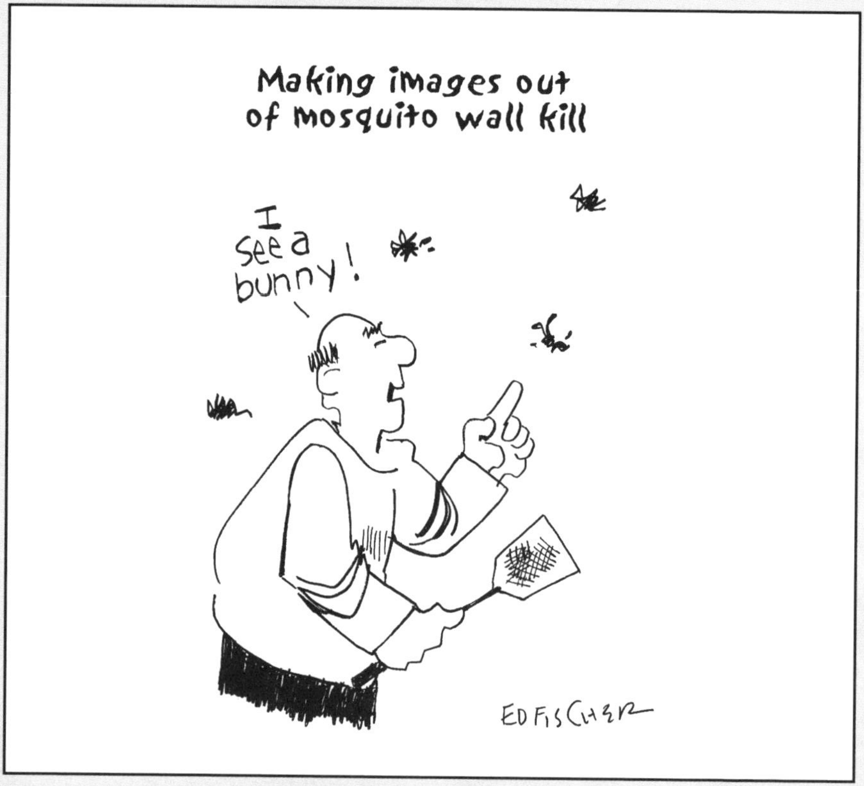
Making images out
of mosquito wall kill
I see a bunny!
ED FISCHER

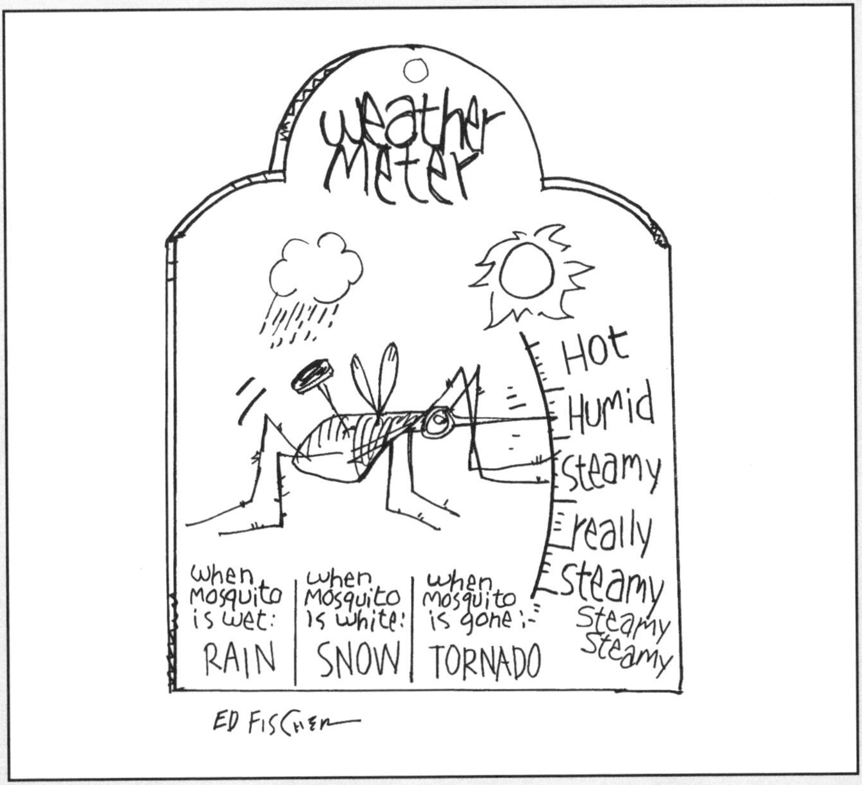

Weather Meter
Hot
Humid
Steamy
really
Steamy
Steamy
Steamy
When Mosquito is wet: RAIN
When Mosquito is white: SNOW
When Mosquito is gone: TORNADO
ED FISCHER

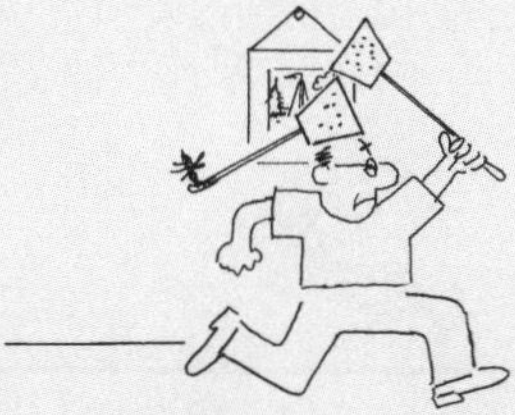

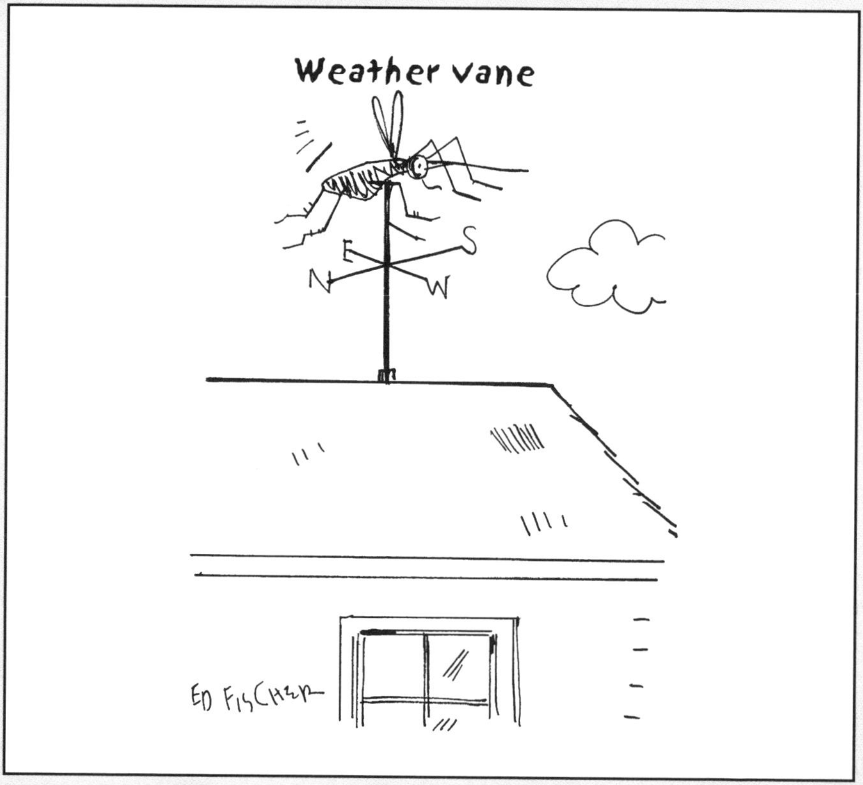
Weather vane
E
S
N
W
ED FISCHER

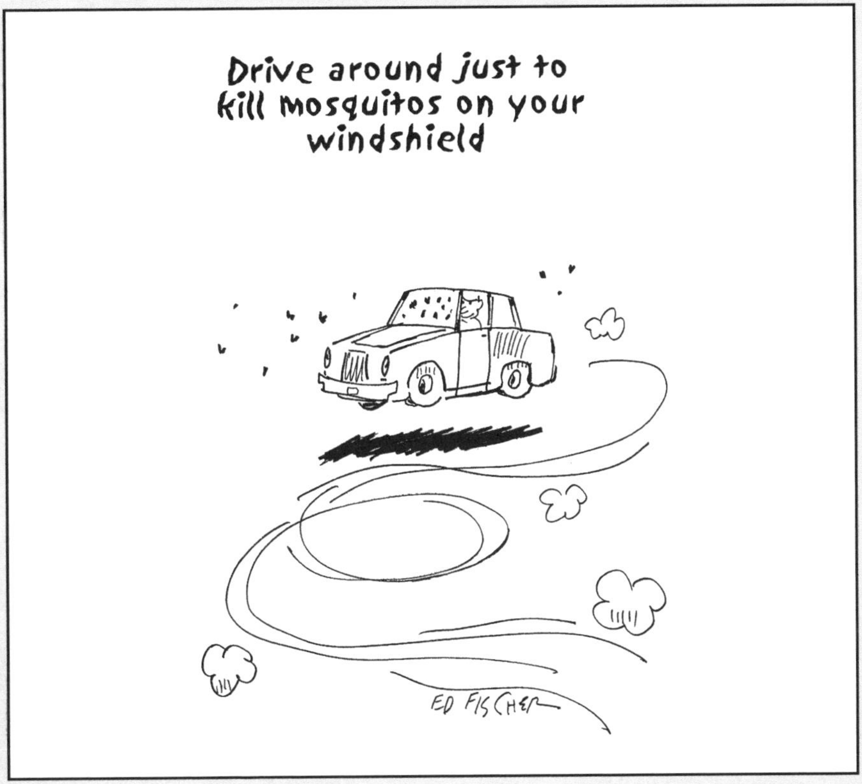
Drive around just to kill mosquitos on your windshield
ED FISCHER

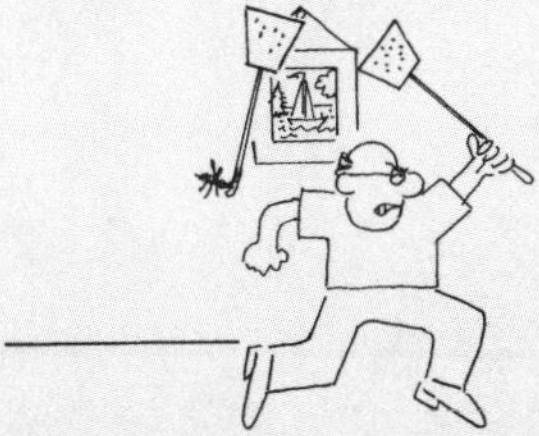

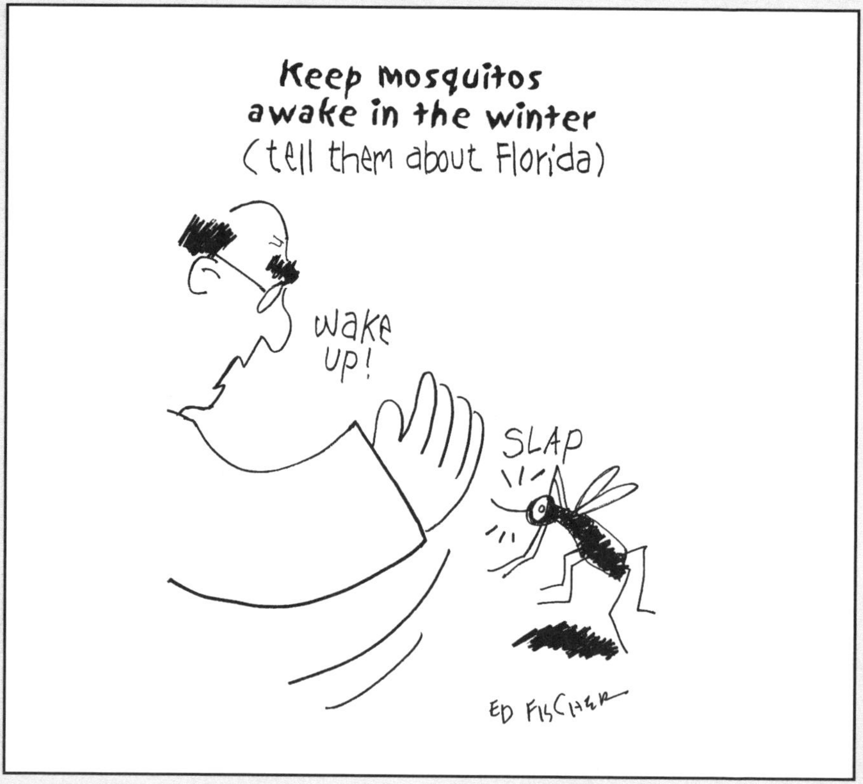
Keep mosquitos awake in the winter
(tell them about Florida)
wake up!
SLAP
ED FISCHER

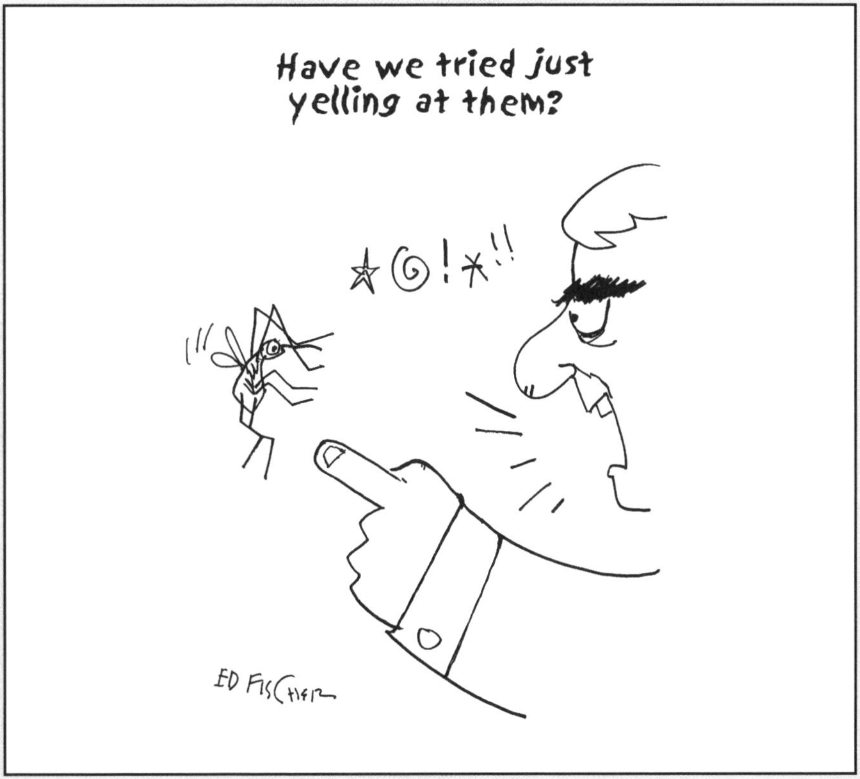
Have we tried just
yelling at them?
ED FISCHER

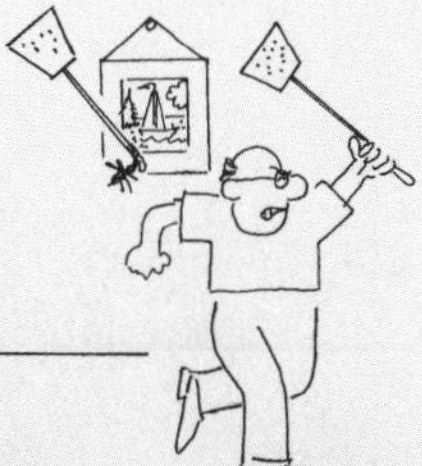

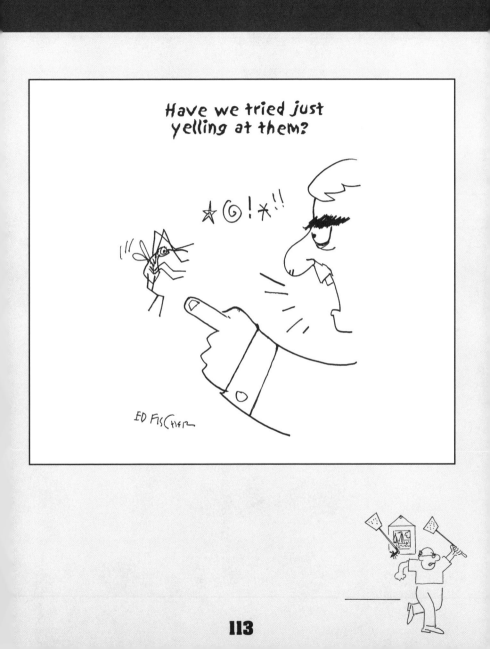

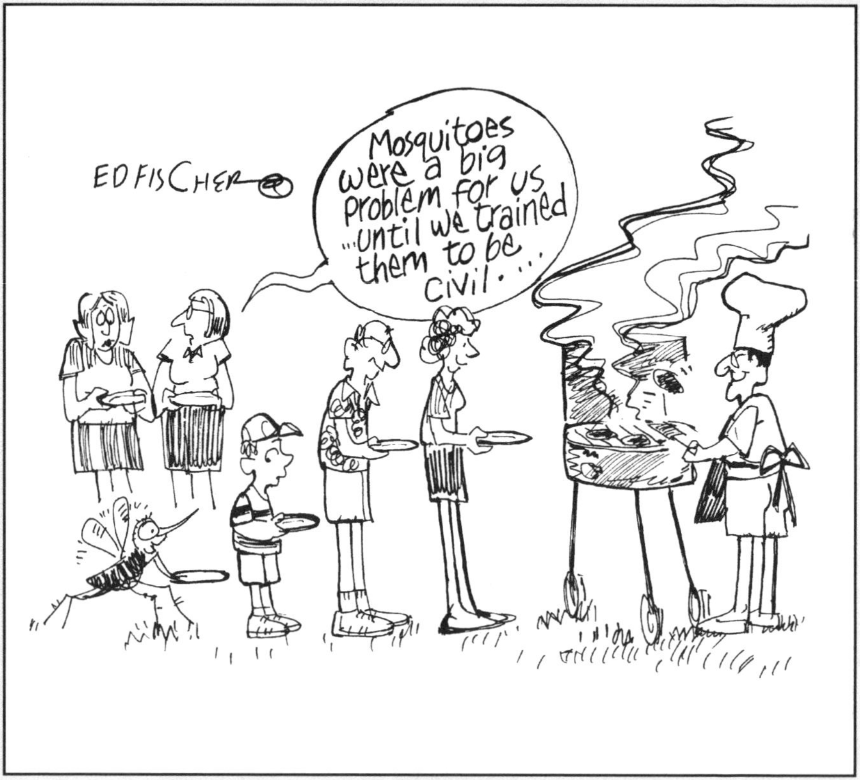
ED FISCHER
Mosquitoes were a big problem for us ...until we trained them to be civil. ...

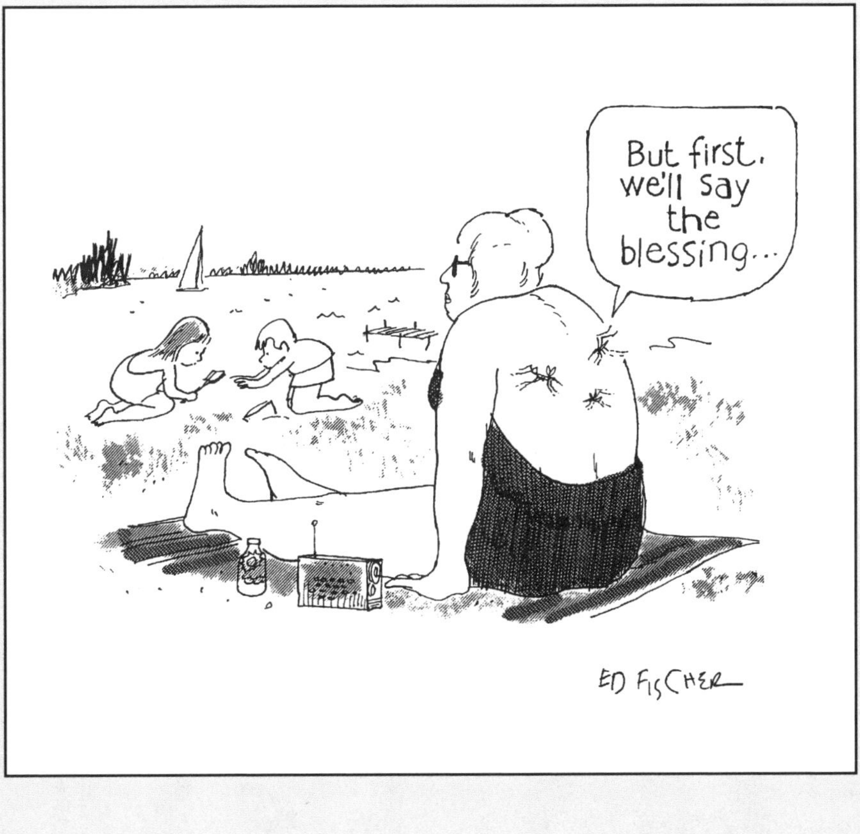
But first, we'll say the blessing...
ED FISCHER

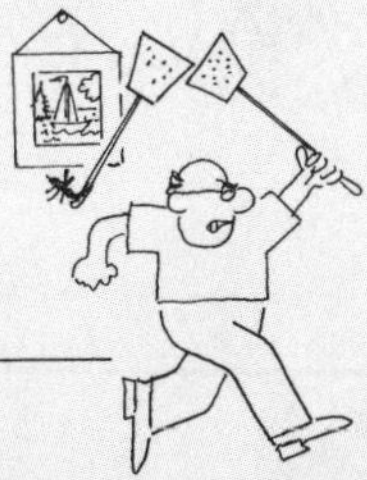

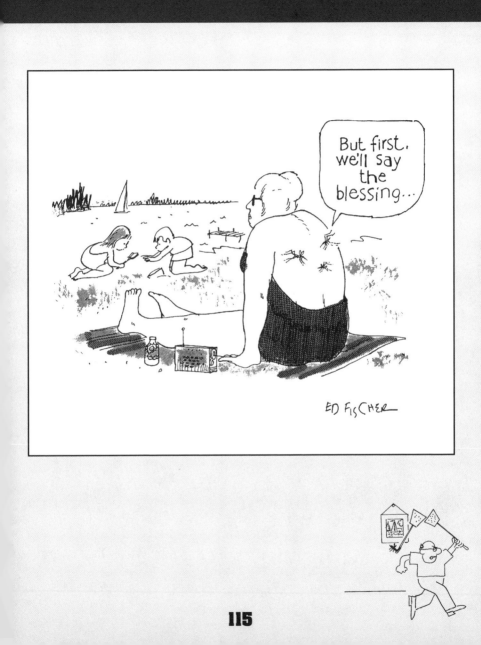

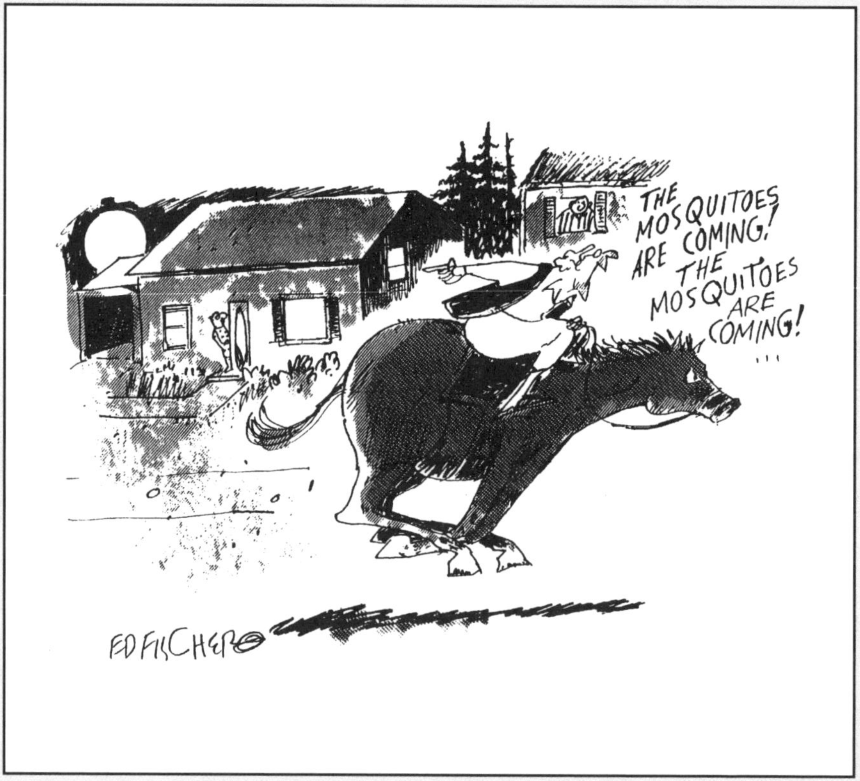
THE MOSQUITOES ARE COMING! THE MOSQUITOES ARE COMING!
...
ED FISCHER

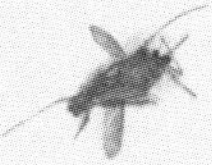

Mosquito Appendix

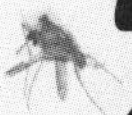

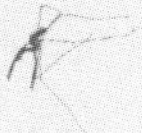

The Good, The Bad & The Ugly

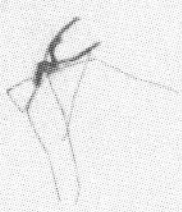

MOSQUITO LIFE CYCLE

As much as we might dislike mosquitoes, we can't help but be impressed with their remarkable life cycle. Depending on the mosquito species, the entire cycle from egg to adult can take anywhere from four days to just over a month. To add a little more excitement, the mosquito's larval and pupal stages can vary depending on temperature: the cooler the temp, the longer the stage. From the start, mosquitoes face an uphill road to make it to adulthood. Water sources dry up, weather conditions might not favor good mosquito populations, predators (including people!) take a toll. But skeeters are designed to survive, and do so in swarms.

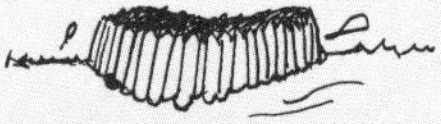

Egg: A female will only mate once, but from that mating she can lay multiple groups of eggs. Once she has mated and found a lucky blood donor, she finds a safe place to hide while her eggs develop; this step typically takes three to five days. Depending on the species, the female will lay eggs directly on the surface of stagnant or sluggish water or on the edge of areas that temporarily flood. If flood waters don't cover the eggs in one season, the eggs will overwinter or even lay dormant for as long as five years. Eggs are either laid singly or in a tidy group called a raft. Rafts can include up to three or four hundred eggs. The eggs hatch in one or two days, and they hatch almost in unison.

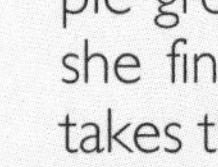

Larva: This stage will last anywhere from four days to two weeks, and it must be a fun time, since the larva's job is to eat. They'll eat anything they can get into their mouths: microorganisms, plant material, other mosquito larvae. The larva moves around quite close to the water's surface, wiggling up to breathe air through a siphon, then resuming the search for food. This activity has earned the nickname wriggler. The larva molts four times, getting bigger with each molt, eventually achieving a length of almost half an inch.

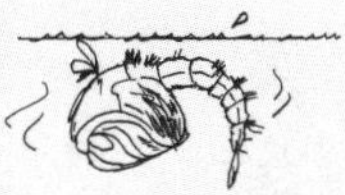

Pupa: The next time a larva molts, it enters the pupal stage. Pupae are called tumblers, again because of the way they move. The pupa will still live fairly close to the water's surface, but it does not eat. The energy that it stored up during its larval stage is now being used to transform into adult form. The pupal stage only lasts a few days; incredible, considering that it is during these few short days that all the larval tissue is transformed into adult tissue.

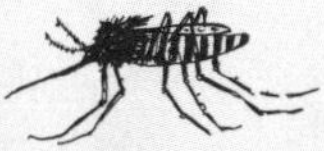

Adult: The freshly minted adult mosquito emerges from its pupal case and rests on top of the water for a while. Once its new body and wings are dried and hardened, it takes off in search of food. In a few days, it will seek a mate and the whole circus starts again.

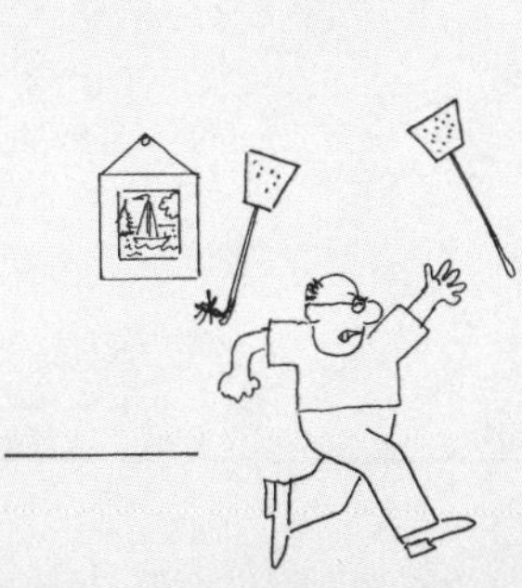

MOSQUITO FUN FACTS

Special equipment

Yes, it's true that you'll only get mosquito bites from the females. Females need the protein-rich blood only to produce eggs. They have special mouthparts with 47 "teeth" to pierce the skin. Males do not have the piercing mouthparts. Both male and female mosquitoes feed on flower nectar for sustenance and the energy they need for day-to-day activity.

There's one in every family

Mosquitoes are in the same scientific order as flies and gnats, an order called Diptera. All members of this order have two wings. The feature that sets mosquitoes apart is that their wings have scales.

Trust me, we're not first on the menu

Mosquitoes have adapted to be able to bite anything with blood. Humans aren't choice hosts, but we are suitable when other hosts aren't available. Different species of mosquitoes prefer different hosts. Some go for small mammals such as your dog, while others think birds are best. Some mosquitoes prefer the particular bouquet of toad, turtle or snake blood.

How many are there? Where?

Of the roughly 2,700 mosquito species that live in the world, only about 200 are found in the U.S. Mosquitoes are incredibly adaptable and have been found at 14,000 feet on the Himalayas and 2,000 feet below ground in Indian mines.

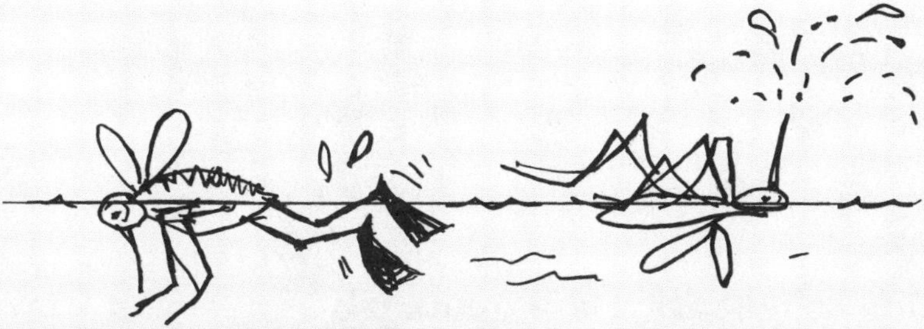

Water is life, literally

Every single species of mosquito requires water to complete its life cycle. The mosquito has a lot of developing to do during its short life: it begins as an egg, then hatches into a larva, then molts to become a pupa, and finally molts again to become an adult.

Just a sip

If a mosquito were to drink its fill, it would still only take one millionth of a gallon of blood (one five millionth of a liter) with each bite. Average adults have between 1.25 to 2 gallons of blood (10 to 15 pints), so would have to be bitten about 1,120,000 times in a short time to be drained of blood.

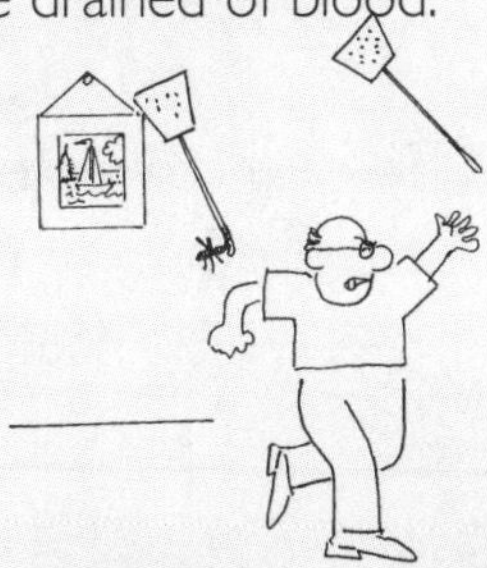

Itchy, itchy

The female needs the blood of her host to flow freely, so when she bites, she ejects a bit of saliva with anticoagulant properties. The itchy bump we're left with is the skin's allergic reaction to the saliva. Some folks are more allergic than others, and individuals can be more allergic to the saliva of certain species of mosquitoes.

Fight fire with fire

Some programs for mosquito control use predatory minnows that feed on mosquito larvae and pupae. Other methods use a light oil to make a coating on top of water. The oil coat clogs the breathing apparatus of the larva and causes it to drown.

The featherweight with the quick jab

On average, mosquitoes weigh in at 2 to 2.5 milligrams. The biggest bruiser tips the scales at 10 milligrams.

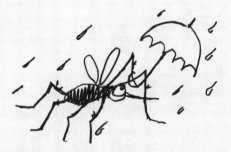

They're nimble little buzzers

Mosquitoes can fly between raindrops. Lucky for them, since a direct hit from a drop could kill.

The good news: you can probably outrun them

Skeeters aren't particularly fleet of flight, typically whining along at 1 to 1.5 miles per hour. The average walking speed of most humans is 2.5 to 3.7 miles per hour.

Sing another sweet one

Mosquitoes can beat their wings up to 600 times per second. Male mosquitoes can find females of the correct species by the pitch of the whine that their beating wings create.

No place like home

The mosquitoes of most species fly within a mile of their hatching grounds for their entire lives. The salt marsh mosquito, found along the East Coast, can migrate 75 to 100 miles.

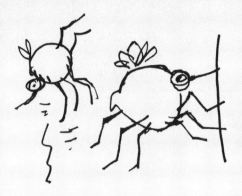

That's cruel!

If the nerve in the mosquito's stomach that tells it when it's full of blood were to be severed, the mosquito would keep sucking blood until it pops.

You can run, but you can't hide

Mosquitoes find hosts by seeing movement, sensing heat from bodies and detecting compounds like increased levels of carbon dioxide and other chemicals our skin naturally produces. Skeeters are more attracted to certain people, but the legion of complexities in this attraction have yet to be discovered. Mosquitoes can "smell" hosts from about 65 to 115 feet away. Once the mosquito has caught your scent, it will usually start flying in a zigzag pattern to follow the chemical trail to its source. When it gets close enough, the mosquito relies more on heat.

Don't they ever sleep?

Some mosquito species are active during the day, others during the night, and others at the in-between times. Chances are if it's mosquito season, there will be mosquitoes around no matter what time it is.

Instructions not included

No single repellent or control method works the same way or as effectively on every species of mosquito. In fact, more than 50 species of mosquitoes are resistant to at least one kind of insecticide.

Hot stuff!

When a mosquito is about ten feet away from its blood donor, it uses thermal sensors in its antennae to find an area where the blood is close to the surface and accessible. When it's really humid, the mosquito can sense the heat from the host at a range of 30 feet.

But only the good die young

Depending on the species and the set of hazards she faces, a female mosquito lives for 3 to 100 days. Males' lives are even shorter: they can expect a life span of 10 to 20 days. Some females can overwinter and may live for as long as six months.

Now that's productive

A single female mosquito can produce an average of 1,000 to 3,000 offspring during her short life.

Serious pest

The diseases that mosquitoes can carry, which include malaria, dengue, yellow fever, West Nile virus and encephalitis, annually kill more than 1 million people worldwide.

You thought zero to sixty in four seconds was fast

A mosquito can go from egg to adulthood in as little as four days.

Want bug bits on your salad?

As tempting as bug zappers might be (oh, the sound of frying mosquitoes), they put only an infinitesimal dent in mosquito populations. Bug zappers will attract mosquitoes, but typically don't kill them. In fact, the ultraviolet light emitted by zappers can actually help skeeters find standing water in which to lay eggs. Unfortunately, zappers attract large beneficial insects as well, and when a big bug hits the zapper, it explodes. The bits of these beneficial bugs then scatter and land on people and food nearby.

Flying under the radar

Foggers and sprayers will send skeeters to the great swamp in the sky, but they also kill the bugs you want to have around: butterflies, dragonflies, praying mantis, even crawlies like earthworms. More bad news is that the generations of mosquitoes that survive the fog will build up an immunity to the chemical in as little as two months.

Smoking section, please

Smoking coils and citronella candles repel mosquitoes by confusing their sensors and hiding your chemical signature in the same way that repellent sprays do.

There's always room for more

To make room for more blood, some mosquitoes will excrete excess water.

Don't mess with Texas

West Virginia has 24 species of mosquitoes, the least number of any state. On the other end of the scale, Texas is home to 82 species of bloodsuckers.

They're more like appetizers

Bats, birds, frogs, bugs and lots of other animals eat mosquitoes. While mosquitoes are an important part of the menu, they're not a crucial food source for any one of these predators.

What's in a name?

A mosquito by any other name would still suck. Spaniards called the mosquitoes musketas, which means little fly, or zancudos, which means long-legged.

Final Word:

A camper in the northwoods for the first time was surrounded by fireflies. "Great," he said. "The mosquitoes are bad enough, but now they have flashlights!"